ACKNOWLEDGMENTS

First of all, thank you, thank you, Hilary Gatehouse, my editor and friend, without whose help this book might still be a file on my Mac. Thank you Hil for your faith and belief in me and for your motion and direction tempered with patience and understanding that empowered me to give wings to these words.

Thank you Lucy for loving and believing in me. Thanks for all your support and willingness to keep seeing the greatness in me. Te amo Mami. Thanks to all my Puerto Rican family and friends. La Isla Bonita. Thank you Jorge, my brother, for always being there for me.

Thank you Lynne. You were always my best friend. Everything we shared helped open me to seeing what I just could not while we were together. Thanks to my beautiful family; Jens, Nish, Mark, Mom, Larry, Lynn, Dean, Bill, and you too Pop, wherever you are now. I know love is unconditional because of you.

Thank you JoMarie for encouraging me to start writing these Seeds for our website. Bless you Sue, your light and friendship in Alaska helped both of us make it through so many dark days. Thanks for pulling me out of my cave to go get a beer together. Dick and Mary, Donna and Chris, bless you. Thank you for giving to me a sense of family and home. Thanks Donna for encouraging me do grief counseling with the kids and parents of Forget-Me-Not. Every time I walked away a little stronger, a little more grateful.

Thanks as well, to all of you who received these "Seeds" in the daily emails that I originally wrote them in. Your feedback, encouragement and support for sharing them has been so big. I have felt all along that I was writing these in direct response to the hope and meaning that you found in them. I am so grateful for my friends at Unity Church of

Mississauga, Ontario, Canada, especially the board members, Anna and all of you who have showered me with your love and respect. Thanks Robert, Kenny, Carol, Mayra and all of my friends I have met through my radio broadcasts. Thank you Mindy for getting me started with the show and Denise, my program director, for giving me everything I needed to succeed.

Thank you, by brother, Garry for letting me be your friend, for taking me into your amazing heart and life, for showing me in the too short time we had together, how to live, schooling me in the long days, weeks and months that you lived while you died. I miss you buddy, but I still see your smiling face.

Thank you, Richard and Kiernan for your loving editing assistance.

And thank you to my teachers, every soul and life I've been graced to meet or shall.

To You, Jesus for guiding me every moment, for holding me while I was begging you to fix me and cursing you for believing in me enough to let me go through what I needed to and for letting me be your man. To Grampa B. for teaching me with your life and your stories instead of your dogma and for placing my hand in His. To Pierre Teilhard de Chardin for opening my eyes to how the Spirit must work in everything. To Eckhart Tolle for saving my mis-identified bacon, helping me realize that I wasn't the story of me that I felt was destroying me. And to Byron Katie, for reminding me of how silly it is for me to be making up horror stories in place of the most beautiful, adventurous moment a soul could ever hope to take notice of and live in.

Wow. I am one blessed fellow.

CONTENTS

INTRODUCTION

"My life is screwed up. It's not working. I don't understand anymore how to make it better. Is there a way out of the noise, pain, mental and emotional stress I keep experiencing? Is there a simple way that just works?" If you are sincerely looking for these answers, then you are ready to go deeper into the questions that can free you. So read on. This book will begin to immediately speak to you like the wise friend and mentor you've been searching for.

These words are a lifeline for those drowning in the failure of their reasoning.

The *Seeds* were planted three decades ago when I began noticing and collecting quotes that went deeper into the reality of my Spiritual Identity, unfolding through my experience of who I was limiting myself as.

In listening to the wide variety of spiritual teachings, I became aware that something was fundamentally flawed in their bases. My inability to follow where they were leading had nothing to do with my commitment and practice. Instead, it had everything to do with my nature and my heart's refusal to be on board with ideas that ran contrary to the flow of my spirit.

The consistent message I got was that in order to become better, I had to accept that I was less than whole in the first place. Likewise, for me and my life to become richer, healthier, fuller, happier or more complete, I had to accept that I was presently poor, sick, empty, unhappy, and incomplete. And how did that fit in with the awareness I had of my essential nature within the perfection of Spirit? It wouldn't wash.

Early on I had given myself to the idea of willingness over willfulness, that is, I had become aware of how little I understood of myself, life and my belief in the possibility of ever grasping this deep chasm of Mystery. I came to see that by turning over my intention to make sense of what I was perceiving, the Orderly Universe, that was creating everything before me, would show me the harmony within the problem I was making of it.

What followed was the collapse of the expectations that I was compulsively absorbed in and substituting for the real experience of just showing up and actually living. My sense of self, derived from career, relationships, expectations and ultimately my investment in self-image degraded to the point where I finally had no choice but to let go of my hopes, dreams and even regrets about them.

I died to the belief in who I had been, along with the whole idea of making a better version of me. And in that death I found myself fully awake in all that remained—the Present Moment where problems have no basis for existing.

So what can this book do for you? First of all, it will take you on your own personal journey into your own awakening, not a standard of freedom raised by other's experiences or expectations. It will take you compassionately by your heart, your mind and your hand into your freedom and your bliss. How?

- By revealing the sublime fruits and unbridled promises that are realized along your journey. That is, how wisdom, effortlessness, joy, freedom, peace-of-mind, dreams and fulfillment show up by themselves.

- By supporting and empowering your natural ability to see how, regardless of your intention and the choices you make, everything you need always shows up fully, and is never lost or taken away.

- By taking you clearly into facing the flaws of your beliefs to notice how these assumptions are keeping you unconsciously affirming what you don't want and unaware of the majesty of what you already have. Your clear sight into this empowers you to responsibly question why you would continue on blindly seeking such narrow, toxic alternatives, instead of claiming the wide wonder and joy of the possibilities that are so evident around you.

- By reacquainting you with the fullness of this present moment journey that you have always been on. Helping you face the shadow that is blinding you with fear and tightening your grip on an identity within a world, though woefully inadequate, is at least familiar.

- And by assisting you in seeing for yourself, the evidence of what is now before you, providing access to a whole world of possibilities that you have no responsibility for creating.

Take this book in small bites, my friend. It is rich in the nutrients that support your awakening and a little bit will go a long way. If you are confused or frustrated by what you are reading, I encourage you to sit in your bewilderment rather than pressing on towards some resolution with your current beliefs. Instead of fighting confusion or even pain, know that it is really a very good sign. It is your attachment to who you are not, and how that has consumed your life experience—your ego reacting to the clear, present opportunity for release.

Old habits can die hard; a part of you fighting for the very ideas that torment you. So, wait and watch, sit and be patient, hesitate and pass on any sense of urgency. You will consistently find that the boat you could only board in your anxious state, will be followed by open passage on a vessel sailing directly into your heart's desire and the most blissful ports of call you could never even imagine.

These pages are far more than sign posts along the way. They are open portals into the return of your innocence. Welcome home.

Acceptance

ACCEPTANCE

I had been suffering intensely over the seemingly inescapable fact that if I didn't get busy providing for myself, I could very likely end up in a state of desperation. The thought loomed menacingly of being homeless; having no resources, living on the street, rummaging through dumpsters for my survival.

I had nowhere to go. All my energy, motivation and intention appeared to be leaking out uncontrollably, in spite of all efforts to contain it. With each passing moment, the evidence of what I was unable to do, was building towards an unacceptable and imminent future. What would I do? What was going to happen to me?

"Dale ... ", the thought emerged. *"What!"* I shot back. *"You know, if you were homeless ... living on the street ... scouring through your surroundings to live ... "* Odd, that I was still able to keep listening.

"If you were there, on the street actually living this way ... you wouldn't be worrying anymore about whether or not it was going to happen to you or how you could avoid it. You would be free of the fear of it, because you would be busy living it."

Suddenly I realized that the end of my compulsive suffering—this intensely incessant self-badgering, was possible. All I had to do was accept that I could and would face whatever life had in store for me.

"You know," I said to the voice. *"I think I'll take that."*

In that moment, the future and the past stopped bullying me and the joy of what I could now see in the present moment became possible. I found lasting peace.

Acceptance is surrender into the Wonder, Delight and Order of Mystery. Without the willingness to accept what is before you, exactly as it is; raw, unqualified, and spontaneously new, your life experience degrades into a monotonous series of familiar actions and hollow results. Through acceptance, longing is allowed to move into fulfillment. When you can accept as complete, what you are misinterpreting as lacking, every person, thing and situation shows up far beyond what you dared dream you might find in them.

A dog barks, the
wind blows, and
what's before me,
just is what it is.
I stop trying to
change what I
think I see and I
am able see more
of what is really
there.

MIND WHAT MATTERS

"Opportunity for most of us, doesn't knock just once; she raps a continual tattoo on our doors. The pity is that much of the time we're either too preoccupied to hear or too lethargic to answer."

... Benjamin F. Fairless

A sure way to fill the mind and subsequently, the heart and body with stress is to automatically give our thoughts over to changing what's before us. Without pausing for inquiry, the unlimited potential of what could be is relegated to the narrow bandwidth of what's to be expected. *"No ill shall be reexamined, nor blessing unjustifiably received."* Says the ego. *"Something must be done about it first."*

What has been, or might be, is the stuff of pure fantasy, and when we choose to pursue this course, we get lost in a convoluted story of our own making. There is a clear way back from this confusion to simple reality. Just see and accept the complete absurdity of compulsively working towards fixing what we've never honestly determined is actually broken.

Peace of mind begins with accepting what is. Everything in our lives has immediate purpose and is self-revealing, but we can only know this if we're present to witness it—not occupied with thinking about what needs to be done.

What if nothing is needed at all and the open door is just behind our own belief in the closed one in front of it?

I listen for when
the Universe
says, "No" to my
intentions. I accept
this necessary
disappointment
as evidence of ripe
and emerging
possibilities that I
have yet to notice.

No, No, A Thousand Times No

"Listen. Make a way for yourself inside yourself. Stop looking in that other way of looking."

… Jalal ud-Din Rumi

When we're holding on to what we want but can't have, sometimes all that seems possible is to feel the pain, keep breathing and wait for help. It's a form of tough love that the Universe continually gives to us as consistently as we try to refuse the offer.

We have no control over others or what they'll do, even when it seems that our intentions appear to match up well. For as quickly as wants change, so does our ability to manage any situation or relationship.

Though we can't control what happens, we do have a lot of latitude for allowing our interpretation of it to change. And it can start from the frustratingly, unavoidable realization that what we're trying to make happen, simply won't. Then we can finally ask the question the whole Universe has been waiting to hear, "If not this, then what?"

We don't have to nag the Universe for what we want. It's always saying "yes" to our desires and giving clear, immediate direction. Pay attention however, when It says "no". It's Spirit's firm way of telling us that we're looking for a door that's already open, but down an alleyway that's closed.

I accept who I am,
what I experience
and where it leads
me. I have faith
in whatever the
moment brings
and my ability to
fully live it.

NOTHING LEFT

"Better a diamond with a flaw, than a pebble without."

… Confucius

It's hard to carry secrets. It takes a moment by moment, 24/7/365 effort to keep them concealed. A part of us is always watching, for fear that, like wild, caged birds, they'll bolt free the second we turn our back. And yet, all the while we're holding tight, they peck and chirp incessantly about the dangers of their possible escape.

It never ends. And, though we learn to seemingly tune out this relentless drain on our energies, it takes a heavy toll in restlessness, disease and suffering. It's the taproot of compulsive thinking and addictive behavior.

Why do we enslave ourselves? So that we'll look like everyone else who's secretly clinging to the same madness.

Someone once asked an aide of John David Rockefeller, upon his death, "What did John D. leave behind?" The reply? "Why, everything, he left behind everything."

Is what we're hiding worth the cost we're paying for continuing to conceal it? What if we just accepted our regrets and lived out the consequences instead? At any moment we would be free to say, "Why, I've left nothing behind. I'm living everything."

*I accept myself as I
am and my life as
I live it. I believe
in my path and
how I am led to
walk it.*

I Believe In Me

"... if at the end, when I come to lay down the reins of power, I have lost every other friend on earth, I shall at least have one friend left, and that friend shall be down inside me."

... Abraham Lincoln

It takes courage to be true to oneself. The pressure to fit in with established norms can feel immense and the desire to be accepted in the presence of another may weigh huge in the balance of choice.

However, making decisions based on the approval of others is a certain formula for disaster and suffering, for in order to do it, we have to abandon and betray ourselves.

Although it may prove wise and helpful to entertain another's input or suggestions, our clearest motivation to action is generated within our own heart's leading, where personal beliefs and convictions are forged from our core values. Thus, we keep in tune with our spirit and at peace in our soul.

Demands from the world change with the wind and it's easy to get caught in and broken by the storms they brew, but by relying on our inner compass for navigation, we're insured a safe trip no matter how raging the seas or loud the clamor to change course or even abandon ship.

Believe in yourself, especially when no one else will. Someone has to stand firm in what you know to be true and for you—it's you.

*I accept myself as
I am and you as
you are. Each of us
has Unconditional
Authority for
expressing our
uniqueness in the
form that it takes.*

HOLD STILL PLEASE

"It is better to be hated for what you are than to be loved for what you are not."

... *André Gide*

Many of us were taught to get along with others. The Golden Rule: *"do unto others as you would have others do unto you"* was our maxim.

The principle, however, is corrupted through lack of self-respect, for we can't give to another what we won't give to ourselves.

Self-acceptance shows us that what other's think about us is their business, not ours. It's how they are unconsciously attempting to see what is hidden inside themselves by projecting it onto others. When this happens it is possible for us to practice the golden rule, by giving others what we would appreciate; an unattached, objective view of what is causing so much frustration. We can be a clear mirror for them. What a gift!

We all disagree on the simplest of things, but does it really matter? Who among us doesn't feel bewildered by the grandeur of life's mystery, yet hopeful when peers model for us confidently, that it's no big deal?

Accept yourself, your uniqueness and confusion. Give others the same respect. Contrary to worldly wisdom, respect is never earned, but always warranted. Each of us is a unique masterpiece, even when we're pretending that we're not.

Appreciation

Appreciation

The conversation during dinner was just getting interesting. By listening, I was able to drop enough of my shields and sacred bias' to hear more of what was being shared, as well as what was left unspoken.

A young man, anticipating the thrill of intellectual swordplay, began plying me with more and more probing questions and countering my responses. Caught up in the joy of mutual exploration, the table came alive with an explosion of shared experiences, personal reflections and heartfelt, crafted understandings.

The silent now spoke, the verbose strained to listen, the walls of generational, social and prejudicial distinctions began to converge. Laughter and intensity, defensiveness and vulnerability, force and compassion, were now dancing around the room in mutual respect; through the eyes and upon the lips of newfound friends.

"So sorry to see you leave Chuck." I, my young friend and my seatmate echoed, as Chuck put on his coat to go. The bond of our new friendship so richly in the air, no further word of love and respect needed to be spoken.

As if an afterthought, he turned to me and said, with almost childlike curiosity, *"I don't know why, but I am feeling anger with you."* Then just as spontaneously he turned respectively to the others and said, *"and I am angry with you and you too. And I don't know why, but that's what I'm feeling."* His pondering this, softly upon his face, was a parting gift of raw, innocent self-revelation.

I felt humbled and speechless in the presence of his offering. The glow of appreciation for the love that we are and how similarly confused we can be in the mystery of our expressing it, said everything.

Appreciation is the state of mind where you see fully. There never is *a this* that is much better than *a that*. There is always so much more to everyone, every thing and every situation. Appreciation is how you see the Whole of Life in what seemed to be only a small part of it.

There's so much
I notice about
the wonder in
you. Now is my
opportunity to let
you in on what I
see.

HAND TO HAND COMPLIMENT

"What this world needs is a new kind of army—the army of the kind."
... Cleveland Amory

It's odd how we can believe that to touch hearts we need to have something prepared to offer, when all it takes is for us to show ourselves as we are.

For nothing, no thing or idea, frees us like honesty and vulnerability. We respond full heartedly to such a gift. It strikes a warm, resonating chord deep at the source of our longing.

Our raw presence awakens the most clear and simple appreciation, childlike in its sincerity and affirming of the most sacred and potent truths ever spoken—the Voice of Two Hearts as One.

I believe in you. I'm so grateful you're in my life. I'm better for knowing you. I feel joy and hope when I'm with you. I'm amazed by how you do that, so naturally, so easily. You're a kind man. You're a tender woman.

I learn so much when I'm with you. I notice how well you do this. I'm aware of how beautiful, lively, attentive, sincere, generous, peaceful, compassionate, courageous, resilient and calm you are.

May I just sit beside you? Hear the life in your voice? I sometimes feel sad, afraid, lonely, confused. I feel better just being near you.

*We're not just
passersby. Much
more is possible.
We can see the
other's glory when
they cannot see it
for themselves.*

Unfathomable Depths

"I don't like that man. I must get to know him better."

… Abraham Lincoln

Judging the world by its cover, it appears to be an unfriendly, disorderly place in need of our best efforts to fix it.

But, before we work our plans, we would be wise to get a clearer understanding of what there is about it that needs change.

We all have a great depth, integrity and spirit that is far more than the surface images we project through casual encounters or cursory examination. To miss this part of us is to trade one single note for the whole movement of a symphony. For life is Masterfully woven from our intentions, confusions and possibilities within a Universe that mysteriously encompasses and integrates all of it together.

The world bears bountiful fruit. It's growing and sustaining itself this moment. And we bring this vision into visibility through our willingness to embrace the human spirit, holding in extraordinary respect every person and living thing that embodies it. Thus realizing that all resistance to full compassion and selfless intention is but *skin deep*—a trivial matter of surface perception and behavior.

Who stands within us and before us is uncovered in the depths that we're willing to mine. Dig a little deeper. There's gold underneath.

*I am here to give
the blessings the
Universe has
placed within me.
Whatever is before
me holds the
opportunity and
inspiration for my
giving it. There is
no mistaking this.*

UNSUNG VALOR
EXTRAORDINARE

"Whoever can weep over himself for one hour is greater than the one who is able to teach the whole world; whoever recognizes the depth of his own frailty is greater than the one who sees visions of angels."

... Isaac of Nineveh

The hero of most novels, movies and other tales is often the strong, silent type who perseveres against all odds unto victory. While this makes for great storytelling, it also sustains the illusion that true greatness is measured by accomplishment. Nothing could be further from the truth.

Rational judgment portrays character by overcoming perceived adversity. Wisdom knows it is the willingness to persist on blindly into the mystery of the sublime unknown.

Among us there are innumerable ordinary heroes, who, without recognition or witness, quietly raise the bar of human sanctity through their performance of those humble deeds that are necessary in this moment.

They move mountains of doubt; holding on when hope seems gone and prospects dim. They persevere against all odds struggling through despair to provide what is needed for themselves and their loved ones. They inspire greatness, daring to believe in something larger than themselves that must believe in them as well.

And they command the full Grace of the Universe taking heart in their plight, fortifying their resolve through the guideposts that regularly appear while bringing to light the promises that can only be realized along the way.

Look in the mirror. Behold the hero.

*I look into your
eyes and see myself.
You are more than
a mirror; you are
my heart looking
back at me.*

SOMEHOW WHEN WE TOUCH

"Cosmic energy is love, the affinity of being with being.. . . The forces of love drive the fragments of the universe to seek each other so that the world may come into being."

... *Father Pierre Teilhard de Chardin*

The desire to belong is a powerful force. It comes from an inner longing to experience with others what we already know to be true inside—that we're all joined at soul depth.

We look out upon the world through the same singular, not similar, portal. Although our being and view is communal, our sense of self is separate, stemming from shared belief and agreement about the individual bodies and experiences we form, attach to and misidentify as our separate selves.

There are moments when we experience the reality of our union: alone within the silence of mind or nature, in the presence of others when our common brilliance dwarfs individual intention, and uncontrollably when disasters occur that shake our psychic ground.

When this happens we act as one because we are and we see that we can. The window of shared experience is visible because our individual agendas and weaponry have either slipped aside or been stripped away.

Nothing can compare to the joy and fulfillment of experiencing our belonging to one another. It's a long desired and awaited homecoming, a joyous, peaceful return from the struggle, confusion and weariness of pretending that we're alone.

*I forgive how I
have misjudged
you, me and
the Universe
that creates and
supports us. I was
simply mistaken.*

No Fault Assurance

"Forgiveness is the fragrance the violet sheds on the heel that has crushed it."

... *Mark Twain*

Forgiveness and humility go hand in hand. Without an understanding of how thoroughly Spirit employs every thought, feeling and action within an orderly and perfected cosmos, all we ever see is how isolated, random events affect our preferences.

It takes awareness of who we really are and who it is that we're relating to in order to forgive. Accepting that the Universe knows what It's doing with all of us, we develop faith in our purpose and how it plays out in existence, irrespective of our expectations.

Within this light the act of forgiveness is elevated from morality to divinity. We realize that to forgive is to admit and accept that our judgment about another or a situation is lacking understanding. So how can we say what is right or wrong when we no longer have faith in our assumptions about how our actions really affect each other or any outcome?

I lose my job to find my heart's service. My finances collapse and I gain security in the loss of my fears about it. Your withholding love turns me toward realizing how deeply I love myself.

How can I say what is bad and what is good? I forgive myself for trying to interrupt the flow of blessings.

Belief

BELIEF

She came to me with pain and hopelessness in her eyes. *"I don't know what to do? Can you help me? I have this situation ... "* and on she continued until she told me the whole impossible tale that was both unique to her and all too familiar to me.

The more I considered the complexity of her situation, the more impotent I realized my reasoning was. She would need help beyond anyone's ability to solve the problem. She would need no problem.

I spoke to her and said, *"Have you considered that this might not be a problem at all, but a calling? Maybe what is presenting itself is an opportunity for you to release the belief in this madness as a dilemma? And is it further possible that you might be in this situation to help others who are caught in this belief, see that you no longer have faith in the replaying of it? Could it be that, by modeling not getting lost in the call of its confusion; unconsciously reacting to what really needs no reaction, you might help them let go of this insanity as well?*

"Is it possible that instead of your being held ransom in this drama, your Spirit is offering you a parting gift to share before you are free to move on?"

She sighed deeply, smiled wistfully and let me know that she suspected she might have gotten what she came for, and that she would sit with her new found consideration of these beliefs.

I pulled up my email today, three weeks later. She wrote, *"Thanks for keeping me grounded! You did say that I could be mistaken about what I was believing and you sure saw the light ... It all took care of itself and I'm moving on. I actually had nothing to do but keep the faith, believing that all would be well ... The Universe is my playing field."*

Have you noticed that most of what you are living seems so truly inferior to what you would really like it to be? This is the result of habitually living what you believe. Beliefs are what you make up and replace your Dreams with, and even at its best it is never fully satisfying. Like small children who peek through their fingers while watching a scary movie, you can narrow your vision to avoid seeing what you believe may threaten your intention. But so doing blinds you as well to your birthright of Creativity that surrounds you in a sea of Blissful Possibility. And besides, you can get so tired of having to keep your hands up in front of your face.

I accept the fear
in my life. I am
willing to meet
it as my teacher
and release it from
protecting me.

ENEMY MINE

"The moment you try to free yourself from fear, you create a resistance against fear. … What is needed, rather than running away or controlling or suppressing or any other resistance, is understanding fear; that means, watch it, learn about it, come directly into contact with it. We are to learn about fear, not how to escape from it."

... *Jiddu Krishnamurti*

Fear can launch us immediately into actions we'd never consider outside their urgency and it can paralyze us as well. We can martial great reserves in reaction to it.

Fear stands guard within our bodies, tenaciously deflecting all wandering or intentioned inquiry into the reality of our beliefs. It censors and sanitizes our interpretations of our past, defending how we came to our decisions about what they meant and still mean.

Fear has been generated to resist all threats to the beliefs it protects. It does so by steadfastly re-stimulating our past memories of the horrid sensations and dire warnings that we unconsciously accepted, in hopes of surviving what was confusing, painful, unacceptable.

Fear is a two-way street. The same supportive intention for survival that conceals and maintains the status also fuels desire for clear discovery and release of the limitations it defends.

We determine if fear will enslave or free us by how we greet it. As a powerful sentinel, it rises to ward off all countermanding intentions and every thrust of change. And like the gatekeeper, it freely initiates the true believer into the sacred chamber where secrets are revealed.

I am the beauty,
joy and wonder
of Being—the
Reality of what
remains when
all efforts to
make something
different cease.

Natural Emergence

"For there is nothing hidden that shall not be revealed and there is nothing covered that shall remain without being uncovered."
  … Jesus the Christ, The Gospel According to Thomas

It's not easy to dwell upon what we don't want in life, but through a lifetime of practice and with peer support, we can get very good at it.

The true nature of life is peace, provision, attraction and full support for every living creation in every situation of every moment. It takes a huge investment of our life energy to deny this ever-present reality, affirming a false front of busyness, poverty, aversion and abandonment as our experience—a 24/7/365 effort.

It's a lot like building a golf course in the desert. Without water being continuously pumped into a place where it doesn't naturally exist, the lush, green illusion expires as the land returns to its dry, natural state.

So it is with our artificially supported beliefs. When we finally come to trusting in ourselves, accepting that we don't want to work anymore at becoming what we're not, we stop replenishing the energy it takes to support this fantasy, and it simply dries up and blows away. What's left is what has always been, a soul perfectly suited for reaping the extraordinary benefits that were there all along.

*I now say yes to
the realization
of my dreams. I
let the Universe
show me how
my thoughts, my
feelings, my actions
and all resources
come together to
make it happen.*

POINT OF CONVERGENCE

"… the moment one definitely commits oneself, then providence moves too. … A whole stream of events issues from the decision, raising in one's favor all manner of unforeseen incidents and meetings and material assistance, which no man could have dreamt would have come his way."
… W.H. Murray from the Scottish Himalayan Expedition

Whenever a dream seems stuck in the wanting stage it's not for lack of resources. What's missing is full intention.

Dreams can and do manifest through a myriad of channels because the universe is ecstatically attractive, inclusive, and diversely creative in expression. Truth is, vehicles and resources for accomplishing any sound purpose are as plentiful as grains of sand.

What is rare and most essential for *making dreams come true* is a commitment to their realization. It's the magnet that attracts everything; the clear lens through which we're suddenly able to see.

It is so simple that we often lose sight of it within the complexity and commotion of our thinking. Whatever is held in mind forms within the world. Sunlight focalized through a magnifying glass sparks fire. Thoughts centered upon one's intention to allow greatness, ignites transformation.

Allow your attention to converge on your commitment. Say *yes* to your dream and your experience in it. Don't bother with the details. They'll come to you. The vision that you find so irresistible is already complete. Yearning only postpones it. Intention starts the party.

*I look to see what
I believe in and
ask myself if it's
true. The truth
of honestly seeing
is the light that is
directly freeing.*

RIGHT LAW,
WRONG APPLICATION

"If you always do what you always did, you'll always get what you always got."

... *Anonymous*

The Law of Attraction states whatever we hold in mind, forms in kind. Creative thinking affirms this principle as the key to improving one's life, increasing health and prosperity and generally getting what we want. However, few achieve what they are conceiving. Lack of effort, feeling and focus generally accepted for the failure.

It takes no effort at all to manifest even the extraordinary. The difficulty is one of blocked intention. We won't let ourselves experience anything that our beliefs are not on board with.

Try applying the Law backwards. Instead of using it to fill in what seems missing, take notice of what, through our present use of the Law, is showing up. Seeing what we believe, we can then question its purpose, what it is costing us and what we might prefer to believe and live instead.

Recurring issues don't change just because we say no to them or have a better idea for dealing with them. Painful patterns dissolve when we finally see how the beliefs that support them, no longer support us.

Fighting against what we are committed to believing in, is insane, no matter how enlightened the weaponry. Looking closely at erroneous beliefs and the absurdity of supporting their tyranny give us no choice, but to release them.

Raise the white flag. It's not your battle.

*I am able to notice
what's going on
inside me—no
change is required.
All I need do is see
the truth of what
is and let that
truth show me the
freedom I have
been missing.*

HEAR MYSELF THINK

"It has always seemed to me a little wishful to say 'I think' or 'I feel.' For the most part, our thoughts think us, our feelings feel us; we do not have much say in the matter. "

… Eknath Easwaran

Imagine living with someone who followed you around ranting nonstop babble in your ear? Would you accept it as a necessary evil, choosing to shut down most everything else in order to ignore the clamor?

Sounds silly doesn't it? But that's exactly what most people do, thinking nothing of what is lost by doing it.

This compulsive noise is the voice of our misguided identification with the sense of who we think we are—the thinker. It rants incessantly, unconsciously masking present reality with frenetic chatter about past recorded events that may or may not have happened. Projecting these memories to effect an imaginary future, it devises a litany of irrational strategies to avoid or improve upon the very stories that it is simultaneously making up.

It goes on unconsciously nearly every moment of our waking and sleeping life without reprieve or renewal of the license we give it to continue.

We don't have to put up with this nonsense. We can take notice of this intrusive badgering, what we are believing about what it's saying, the abusiveness of its delivery and the insanity of our generating it.

When we see the liar and its threats for what they are, we are free to take a stand. *"No thanks, I'll take my chances with raw, live reality over tortuous, convoluted reasoning."*

Courage

COURAGE

"So let me get this straight." He repeated. *"You just stand up before an audience, without notes or any indication at all as to what you are going to say ... and trust that something that people will want to hear will come out of your mouth?"*

"Yes." I said. *"That's about the size of it."*

"I can see where that would take a lot of faith, but how on earth do you manage the courage to actually step out on that ledge?"

"It's a funny thing about courage." I explained. *"It seems like an awfully big word whenever I think about using it to overcome fear, but when I'm just acting on it, it feels so easy and natural, like the only thing to be doing."*

People demonstrate extraordinary amounts of courage every day without ever realizing the fortitude and dauntless spirit they embody and express in doing so. By meeting the situations that demand immediate attention, they simply act courageously, taking no pause to reflect on the audacity of their willingness to so selflessly respond.

A single mother resolutely provides for her family, determined to meet every seeming challenge that life throws at her.

A weathered and beaten man pushes his cart along the street, inspecting every repository of refuse for discarded food and treasure.

A student pushes aside her doubts, enlisting help to understand the materials and concepts that will help her pass her exam and follow her dreams.

A desperate soul, tortured by the nonstop thoughts and feelings that scream of needed change, broken dreams and harsh self-judgment, lives one more moment into some hope of relief.

Right now you take one more breath and one more step in the direction that lies before you, regardless of the uncertainty that dogs you, and the fear of a past and future bullying your intention to simply follow your heart.

What courage, what strength, what a hero you are. If you take the time to notice, you will inspire yourself.

Courage is what you personify when you don't have the luxury of thinking about your fears. It is the magnificence within you that is revealed as you are called to respond to uncertain circumstance; whether large or small, real or imagined. Courage is your nature. There is no avoiding it. And in honestly noticing how you walk your talk, there is no denying the evidence of its footprint upon your path.

*I am made of
the stars, clothed
in Universal
Substance and
given direction
through Infinite
Love. I am the
gleam in the
Creator's Eye.*

BREATHTAKING PERFORMANCE

"Life only demands from you the strength you possess. Only one feat is possible--not to have run away."

… Dag Hammarskjold

Being human isn't easy. It's to be the artist who forms, colors and gives texture to an enthralling masterpiece without losing perspective and oneself within the frame.

Attachment by misidentifying ourselves with our experience has been a necessity of our spiritual evolution, but the cost of this in pain and sorrow has been staggering.

Every soul who has ever worn this skin has not only been courageous, but heroic to angelic proportion. We've struggled on, clinging to the hope of our greatness, in spite of the innumerably confusing, painful and self-sabotaging ways by which we've blindly followed our highest intention to express our perfection.

Billions of lives groping restlessly through millenniums of existence just to realize true nature—could there be any sane reason not to forgive our selves over our confusion? We have borne the spark of creation inside us from day one, radiating the light within while waiting in the shadows of our uncertainty, faithfully carrying this mysterious flame to the moment of fruition.

More than mercy is warranted. The Universe stands in awe of our achievement.

I challenge every belief that tells me doors are closed. I want to examine them for myself.

QUESTION CERTAINTY

"I will not die an unlived life.... I choose to risk my significance; to live so that which comes to me as seed goes to the next as blossom and that which comes to me as blossom, goes on as fruit."

... Dawna Markova

One of the least examined, most tenaciously held beliefs human beings cling to is that we're better off continuing on in what is difficult and stressful, rather than trusting in ourselves enough to let go into the promise of finding something better.

This entrenched belief is fortified by our unconscious acceptance of a false sense of memory that seems to justify irrational fears. We can't quite identify when it was that we actually tried to let go and failed, but we're certain that we did and that it was disastrous. *"Don't even think about it!"* the mind threatens.

So here comes the million dollar question: Do we know it's true that holding on to what causes us to suffer is a wiser course than exploring what else might be?

Relationships, situations and all conditions are what we expect them to be. There's no luck involved—it's pure attraction. So, if what we're getting is what we don't want, we can change it by releasing our expectation of it. Start by questioning the belief that tells you to hold on to poor circumstance, *just in case*, because until you let go, *it's always the case*.

I am the author
of my experience.
When my story
seems to repeat
itself, I turn
within to Source
and watch how
my tale unfolds
in new, creative
ways.

OPPORTUNITY TO HEAL

"Your living is determined not so much by what life brings to you as by the attitude you bring to life; not so much by what happens to you as by the way your mind looks at what happens."

... *Kahlil Gibran*

The world is moving. Something happens reminding us of what happened before, a situation we remember having no control over. We tried to shape it into something we could manage and through frustration, guilt, anxiety we somehow got past it.

Yet now, the same sense of urgency, powerlessness and frustration has risen again, along with the resentment and shame for having to relive and react to the same troubling experience.

Now is the time for healing. We begin by loving ourselves, acknowledging that we are entitled to take these few moments to minister to ourselves, free of the stress pressing upon us.

We close our eyes and relax, sensing our body, noticing from within that we have one and how it feels right now. With everything going on around us, our body is happening as well.

As we sense our body and our breathing, we notice how we watch everything and we can see that we're not caught in any situation, or subject to it. We breathe into the world, trusting and allowing what is happening to naturally reshape.

Something is never what we think it is. It's always so much better when we give life the chance it needs to show us.

I have the power
to face the shadows
and I am not
afraid to use it.
I bring light and
new beginnings
into all that seems
dark, dire and
concealed.

Big Dogs

"Life is too short to be small."

… Benjamin Disraeli

Years ago I lived with two small Shih Tzu dogs, Tai and Chi. When my wife and I would travel we would board them with a friend who had four similar dogs. Our friend would housesit other breeds, one of which was a large Rothweiler named Lily. Rothweiler's are a powerful breed with tremendous leg and jaw strength that can intimidate even the most confident person.

However, Lily was beside herself, cowering in the midst of these yelping little canines. She had the potential to stand her ground, but she didn't. She sensed they were bigger than her.

We can and often do take the same stance by identifying ourselves with our minds—forming complex, psychological senses of ourselves that portray us as damaged, weak and small. We can believe ourselves to be imprisoned within these small personalities, thus shackling our potentiality.

However, there is no real basis for enslaving ourselves to disease, depression, poverty or any negative condition—only a false, fragile self-image that seeks to conceal the sheer magnitude of our presence.

We're big dogs on this planet. We don't have to worry about what comes nipping at our feet.

*I am courageously,
gratefully alive
and free. My
Being has
dominion over
anything that
could ever appear
in the world.*

UNYIELDING RELEASE

"The words 'I am ... ' are potent words; be careful what you hitch them to. The thing you're claiming has a way of reaching back and claiming you."
... A. L. Kitseman

Addiction, depression and suffering don't point towards defect or limitation; rather they are profound evidence of one's innocence and expansive nature.

It can be difficult to grasp this awareness largely because of shared misconceptions about who we truly are and how pain and suffering relate to our resistance toward unyielding realities.

No one is or has a physical, mental or emotional being, only an experience thereof. We aren't addicts, healthy or disturbed psychological beings or any conditioned self. Each of us is pure, unadulterated Being and yet most still identify with some lesser sense of who we think we are, usually in a state of becoming. But pretending to be our changing experience doesn't make it so anymore than sitting in the wind makes us a breeze or a hurricane.

Identifying with anything instead of simply Being, creates pain, stress and unconsciousness. Our thoughts, emotions and bodies speak to us through feeling, sensation and condition about who we are not (resistance) and who we are (acceptance).

When does suffering end? When the mystery of what could be, opens us to question the cost of living what's always been . . . and fear no longer gets a vote.

Curiosity

CURIOSITY

As she walked out of the mall and across the parking lot, she noticed panic in the woman directly ahead. Pacing, spinning and flailing her arms about, the woman's whole demeanor was a bright flare scorching across the cold, drab sky.

"Are you in trouble?" Sandra asked.

"Yes!" she cried. *"I've locked my keys in my car!"*

"Well, let's call someone to help you." reasoned Sandra.

"No! No!, I can't!" she anguished, *"Do you have a cell phone? I don't and I'm afraid to leave the car. My purse is open, lying on the seat. Someone might steal it if I leave?"*

"I don't have my cell phone right now, but I could wait here while you go call inside or I could leave and call for yo ... "

"No!" she panicked. *"I don't know what to do! Please don't leave me. I'm afraid something bad might happen. Would you stay with me please?"*

"What can I do?" Sandra reasoned with herself.

"Just stay with me!" She cried out more urgently. *"Stay with me until ... I don't know."*

"But, what can I do?" pressed the argument in Sandra's mind.

"Please don't leave me!" The woman begged to herself.

"Yes. Stay with her." A voice of calm assurance settled in upon Sandra's confusion.

"But, but, what can I do?" Sandra reasoned. *"She won't move. I can't calm her. She won't let me call for help. What can I do?"*

"Just stay with me, please, until I can think ... "

"Yes, stay with her." The voice spoke again, reassuring Sandra.

"OK. OK. I'll just stay with her." Sandra finally agreed with herself. *"I don't know what else to do."*

Together they waited ... without knowing what more they could do.

Suddenly the voice spoke to Sandra, *"What are you holding in your hand?"*

"My car key," Sandra thought.

"Try it." Encouraged the voice.

Without thinking she inserted her key into the lock of the woman's car door … turned it … and it opened.

Curiosity is your childlike trust in the Ever Present Wonder of what you have yet to see in what's right before you. It is the delightful attitude with which you act upon faith, with the intention and promise of experiencing greater Joy. Curiosity is what turns *anything's possible* into, *"hey, look at that"*.

*I am passionately
curious about
what's before me,
what more it can
show me and how
I am able to see it.*

PASSIONATELY CURIOUS

"I have no special talents. I am only passionately curious."
                                          ... Albert Einstein

My Grandfather was a master at finding four leaf clovers. When I would walk with him in search of the rare sprout, my doubts of finding one we're always confirmed, but he never walked away from a patch of green without one in hand.

Inspiration and passion for living are linked to discovering what we've yet to notice that is right before us. It piques our curiosity and stirs the imagination, attracting more of the same.

But when we view life expectantly from the familiar we screen out new possibilities. Defaulting to the unconscious, filters out everything except what's predictable, even if it's not what we want. Prayers, affirmations, visualizations—all treatments to expand the prosperity of experience—run head on into this cognitive barrier.

Curiosity is the simple, direct way out of this dilemma. By exploring *what could be possible* we automatically free ourselves from *what seems most likely to happen.*

Let go of the predictable question—*"Is this what I think it is?"* The answer is always, *"No!"* Release your passion to inquire more curiously, *"What more could there be?"* Change your perspective and you'll turn everything inside out. Who knows, maybe you'll find one with five leaves.

I am heartened
within the
darkness, knowing
that my fear
and confusion
lead precisely to
where with the
faintest inner
light, my most
grievous errors are
redeemed.

The Last, Best Hiding Place

"An age is called Dark, not because the light fails to shine, but because people refuse to see it."

… *James Michener*

It's not unusual to fear the darkness. Children and adults alike avoid it.

A few years ago during a men's retreat a group of us explored a cave deep within the earth. When settled inside, our leaders turned off their flashlights, and for a number of minutes we sat still within total darkness. We were prepared for the experience, yet immediately the rising fear of having lost my reliance upon everything familiar pressed urgently upon me.

Ironically, our greatest fear of outer darkness and complete hopelessness is an opening to our greatest joy of inner light and full faith. For darkness of thought, whether in a cave, a relationship or an illness, shines light on the fraudulence of the concealed beliefs that we bully ourselves with.

Darkness isn't real. Light is. Even a small crack, allowing light to pour in, will expose everything. What's easily visible becomes hidden when we block out the Light Source. So to see the Light of Truth and the wonders it offers us, we need only release our grip around the beliefs that are shielding us from seeing it.

Shine your light into the dark places you fear. Every shadow covers treasure like a blanket.

*I'm here to give
birth to heaven on
earth, not a better
rendition of my
personal perdition.*

Daybreak, Sunsets, Me

"Everywhere I go, I find a poet has been there before me."
... Sigmund Freud

The Majesty of Spirit is evident in the painting of a beautiful sunset, the structural genius of a beehive, and the spectacular canyons carved from the flow of rivers. Yet, when it comes to finding our place in this natural world we imagine that all this perfection has bypassed us, forcing our hand to find another way.

How would a spider web, the Northern Lights or a whale's spout appear if the Universe gave humankind the task of creating them? They might appear as immaturely distorted as does greed, self-interest and callousness in representing generosity, altruism and compassion.

Humankind is awakening to its silent, still nature and the cost of our continued fixation upon the mental noise that drives us. We're witnessing a growing awareness of the utter failure of our schemes to conceal the glaring flaws within our intentions, along with an expanding joy and gratitude for the whole, new possibilities that are presenting themselves in the emptiness of old, broken promises.

We're in the place now where we can feel the peace of perfection streaming through our minds, in the absence of the noise that we used to fill it with.

*I have a childlike
capacity for joy,
wonder and
discovery. The
world is new and
fresh for me today.*

TEST DRIVE IT

"The life which is not examined is not worth living."

... Plato

The secret of life is actually seeing it. Nothing more is necessary. Life is beautiful and full as it is ... no matter what it is. However, we can't experience this if we won't take notice of it.

Small children have no problem with this. They examine everything in their environment, sensually, for the sheer enjoyment of what's right before them. They don't have the time or intention to think about what it all means, being far too absorbed in the investigation.

We adults tend not to observe life with the intention to discover, but to mediate and classify it; impressing the memories of our previous experience upon what is freshly before us. We call this *giving it meaning*. We see life only long enough to recognize it for what we *think it is* and by then we've stopped looking; occupied with thinking about what we *believe it to mean*. All the while life is erupting into a panoramic display of wonder that we could enjoy if we weren't so distracted by thinking about what we *think we saw*.

Enjoy life. Accept and expect that whatever it is, it's nothing you've ever seen before. Now, pick it up and take a closer look.

*I am immersed
in the delicious
sensations of my
surrounding
reality. I savor
the field trips that
turn book reports
into prose and
poetry.*

I'm All Wet

"Argue for your limitations, and sure enough they're yours."
… Richard Bach

We can see life as it is or as how we want it to be. This is the power of the mind and why all human experience is unique.

Our minds have two modes of operation; observing or reflecting.

The former is what young children use almost exclusively in their intention to sense and discover their surroundings. Through sight, sound, smell, taste and touch they know the world through their immersion in it.

The latter mode is what most adults use almost exclusively in their intention to catalog and objectify their surroundings. By recalling the past and projecting its meaning into the future they step back from their world in order to rationalize and reform it.

We can't observe and reflect at the same time. When we sense our surroundings, our thinking shuts down and by thinking about anything, we close ourselves off from the sensation of it.

Likewise, immersing ourselves sensually in anything opens us to greater discovery of it, while objectifying the same, at best, forms a less objectionable or more pleasing facsimile of yesterday's news.

It takes more than an atlas and water sample to know a river. You've got to get close enough to get wet.

Freedom

FREEDOM

As a young man I explored the thrill of living close to the edge. Like many of my peers, I experimented with sex, drugs, activism and other restricted expressions of my generation.

I bought a motorcycle and, along with riding buddies, discovered the joys of back woods roads, greasy spoons and small town America. In the excitement of my newfound freedom I also started to develop an attitude of privilege and exception; believing that many of the rules of society might be best served applying to someone other than me.

It didn't take long for my actions to come into conflict with society's understanding and enforcement of these laws. I was in the habit of speeding excessively and popping wheelies on my bike on public roads. I soon amassed enough tickets to take my license away, but that hardly slowed me. One day I got caught driving without my license and the judge, looking over my recent driving record, decided a lesson was in order. He sentenced me to ten days in the city jail.

I was going to jail.

The night I was to report in to begin my sentence was the most frightening experience in my young life. The jailer walked me to the cellblock; a large, open, barred in area with individual cells in the back. He opened the gate and directed me in. The heavy sound of the bolt Sealing the door shut jarred me to the reality of my fate.

There were twenty or so older men milling around inside, glancing at me with no particular interest or care. I moved over to a common bench table and sat. I was so scared I couldn't think or feel. I felt absolutely numb.

As if on cue, an older man came over, sat down and started talking with me. I can't remember what he said to me. I only know that whatever it was, his words and manner were kind and the three hours before lights out passed quickly and uneventfully.

Like many new situations in my life, those first few hours set the tone of my experience.

I soon discovered that jail was not the horror that I imagined it would be. The men inside and those who kept them there were human beings like me, with lives, stories and the need for human connection, like anywhere I had ever been from schools to the workplace. We joked, laughed, complained, worked and sat silently together.

For ten days my life didn't stop. I just lived it in a new place. And when I was released, I walked out feeling everything from the joy of returning to a world taken from me, to the regret of saying goodbye to a world I had just received.

I was locked in jail, but I had been free the whole time I was there.

Freedom is the realization that no matter what is happening in the world, nothing affects **you**, (the Being you are and know within), outside of your reaction and attitude about it. Imprisonment ends when you no longer lock yourself up with the thoughts, reflections and stories about what you believe is happening. When you don't know what is happening, then you are completely free to discover it.

The winds of
change are
blowing freely.
When reason
demands that I
secure all hatches,
I climb on the
deck and open the
sails.

SAFE PASSAGE

"And yet, hope pursues me, encircles me, bites me; like a dying wolf tightening his grip for the last time."

… Frederico Garcia Lorca

As a young man the thrill of discovery was my bread and butter. I reveled in the exploration of California beaches, new highways and byways, fascinating watering holes, diverse personalities, the power of money, the allure of sexuality and a myriad of sensual, inspirational experiences.

Gradually though, a change had come over me. After years of seeming slumber I awoke to realize that I had allowed a compulsion for security and its task-mastering to supplant my spirit of adventure so thoroughly that I couldn't feel the sheer joy I had known in its practice.

I saw that I had confused the spontaneity of raw experience with the temptation to cultivate and classify it. I had lost my way.

My story might have progressed on tragically into a broken spirit or heroically through resolve to restoration. It did neither.

The road of adventure has always been firmly beneath my feet. The same spirit that had evoked awe and deep humility in the presence of a moonlit tide or rapture of a first kiss also carried me through the grievous loss of the person I had hoped to become, into the joyous freedom of who I am.

And so along the path I gratefully wander.

*I am content
with the notion
that who I am
shows up best in
the mystery of
what might be. I
choose uncertainty
with suffering
over familiarity
without bliss.*

Consider The Unconsidered

"If you do not expect the unexpected you will not find it, for it is not to be reached by search or trail."

… Heraclitus

How spontaneous and ridiculously fulfilling could life be if we simply chose to pause and question the knee jerk beliefs that habitually serve up the same old life experiences?

What could happen if we entertained the idea that the rules of life could expand into ones far friendlier and more delightful than our expectation of them?

What if it's only our insistence upon guarding an eyedropper's worth of understanding of what's realistic and probable, that keeps us from playing in oceans of infinitely imaginative possibilities?

What if who we are is so magnificent and capable of such clear, unrestricted expression, that in order to even momentarily forestall its evidence and influence, we have to nearly deplete the depth of our vitality in mustering the thought force to do so?

What if the consequences of stepping outside the confinement of our fear, and moving in the direction of our dreams, were not effects at all, but an ever-widening awareness and desire expressing beyond our highest vision.

What if then could be now? What might happen?

I am far too busy
to worry. There
are just too many
rocks to turn over
and ladybugs to
catch.

CHILD'S PLAY

"It takes a long time to become young."

... *Pablo Picasso*

I began counting my birthdays backwards this year. I'm counting down from one hundred and five, so that makes me, well, younger.

It makes sense. The longer I live the more I realize how little life demands and how much it tickles. It's taken many years of near terminal seriousness to learn some of the basics:

- More stuff means more managing of it.
- Being alone can mean I get my full attention.
- Whenever I think something's wrong with me—I'm wrong.
- What people have that I might want, i.e. money, sex, position, influence, attention, is less attractive than their willingness to let me know them.
- Today is so ripe for the picking, who cares about yesterday or tomorrow.
- If I don't know where I'm going, I'm surely in for a surprise.
- And just when I think life couldn't get any better, a new ice cream truck turns the corner.

So I'm a day younger this morning. When I tell friends, they laugh and think it's cute. And I'm laughing too, because, yes, it's a silly child's game. Excuse me please. I'm done writing. I want to go outside and play now.

*I am living in
a world filled
with the joy of
new possibilities
and delightful
surprises. I am free
now to explore.*

STORY TIME

"Row, row, row your boat, gently down the stream. Merrily, merrily, merrily, merrily, life is but a dream."

... *Children's Nursery Rhyme*

It's not what we know that brings us joy but what we discover. What's familiar can soon become dull and routine, limiting our experience to the small sphere of what has been or most likely will be.

Everything was new to us as children. We learned the joy of sensory exploration because it was the only game in town. We had nothing to compare a swing set or doll house to, so we immersed ourselves in them with no critical thoughts pulling in the reins. Every day was a new beginning. Every object and situation had secret compartments.

What has happened since then?

Have we deceived ourselves into believing that somehow we've explored it all and run out of surprises? Like hamsters in a string of cages; could we be so busy that worlds beyond the routine don't seem to exist anymore?

Who would we be if we threw open the door and ran out into open fields? It's no secret why children like to be read to. To them, fairy tales aren't make-believe, they're confirmation of the worlds they've explored today.

Lie back and rest from your busy day ... Let me tell you a story ...

*I am rich beyond
measure. I realize
that empty I
entered this world
and empty I shall
leave it. I am now
free to do anything
I desire.*

SEEKING MY FORTUNE

"I have no money, no resources, no hopes. I am the happiest man alive."
... Henry Miller

In one of the folk tales from the Southern Appalachians, a character named *Jack* goes off to *seek his fortune.* He tries to follow the ways of the world by working on a farm for seven years. Carrying with him a huge bag of coins, he continues on with his journey, entering into a series of trades to reduce the effort it takes him to care for what he now owns.

A simple man, Jack sees that everything he possesses is slowing him down from *seeking his fortune.* People he meets along the way are more than willing to help him reduce his load and he eventually ends up with nothing more than a nail-straightening rock.

Fatigued from his journey, he leans over a well to quench his thirst and accidentally knocks the stone into the well.

"Well," he exclaims looking downward, *"I must be the luckiest man alive. I had a heavy bag of money to carry, then a horse to lead, then pigs to prod, chickens to chase and a nail-straightening job. But now I guess I'm the luckiest man ever, because I don't have anything to keep me from seeking my fortune."*

What's in the way of you *seeking your fortune?*

Grace

GRACE

Friends ask me, *"How do you know that the course you are taking is the right one?"* The answer is so simple it escapes them. *"I know it's appropriate because it's the course I'm taking."*

For most of my first fifty-seven years I lived in the illusion of needing to make the right choice. I believed that this was the point of life, to learn how to make the right decisions and follow through on them.

It never worked, that is, even my greatest achievements never led to the lasting joy and freedom that I was doing it for. In fact, more often my failures brought peace; in the moments between those dashed expectations and gearing up for the next ones, I just accepted what I hadn't been able to accomplish.

Now I know that when facing what's before me, there are only two possible choices I can ever make; either continue making choices or not make any choice at all.

To make a choice about what's before me is, first of all, to arrogantly believe that with my limited understanding, I know more about what Life is presenting me with, than what it can show me. So it then follows that there is no point in noticing what more I might see, or setting aside my preferences to even do so.

Choices always involve the death of all ideas other than what we choose, and they are so high maintenance. *"I should do this over that. Then if this happens, I'll do that, or if that happens I'll do this. I must decide how you and this situation supports, detracts, or delays me and what I need do to make it all work. And how effectively am I following through on the choices I've just made?"* It never ends. And what does it really do for me that truly makes me happy?

In being willing to see the truth of what Present Moment Awareness has to reveal, I have found sanity, and now realize that my story about what is going on and what I should do about it is clearly insane.

It has changed everything. Now I see the movement of Grace upon everything and everyone through ease and joy of experience. So why would I want to make a choice about whatever Life has to offer me, when all my options are versions of the same, old reworked thinking that have always required so much from me, for so very little in return.

I have made my choice. I either say yes to what is before me or wait until yes appears.

Grace is the safety net around all of your life experience, that allows you to discover wonder and magnificence in everything. It supports your every thought and action in deep, true benevolence. As you learn to trust in it, you see that it helps focus and direct your perception. Like a shorter and shorter leash upon your mind's wandering, it Harmonically leads you toward your highest realization and away from all unnecessary drama, distraction and pain. It's better than win-win. It's never losing.

*My light is ever
bright. When it
seems smaller,
it's because I'm
learning how
to brighten a
larger sphere. I'm
discovering how
truly capable I
am.*

HOPELESSLY UNDER GRACE

"Nothing can be attained without suffering but at the same time one must begin by sacrificing suffering."

... *G.I. Gurdjieff*

I believed something was wrong in me, fighting against depression and compulsivity for so long. I had faith in God healing me, but feared I might not survive the cure.

I read of those who'd suffered and ultimately collapsed, freeing themselves from their confusion into a great peace. I tried to force my surrender only to deepen my hopelessness and pain.

Then one day I realized, that while still feeling great angst, I was no longer trapped inside it. I was out walking in the sunlight.

I can hardly believe now, how arrogant my belief was, that the same Force that had miraculously created me, had somehow forgotten me.

No matter who you are or how long, deep or complex your suffering seems, I and others know the path of hopelessness that you now travel. It tested us and now it is our great joy to share with you how utterly we failed to remain deserving victims. In spite of our every toxic thought and act, our Spirit irresistibly freed us.

Your courage is immense. Your faith to carry on for one more moment is heroic, far affecting and more influentially inspiring than we can possibly share. Hang on brave heart. Help is underway.

I accept who I am, who you are and who we are together. I don't know the answers but I am willing to live the questions with you.

NAKED & INNOCENT

"Is it so small a thing
To have enjoy'd the sun,
To have liv'd the light
In the spring,
To have lov'd to have thought, to have done?"

... Matthew Arnold

A newborn, and an adult accepting the approach of death have something in common; they both have little to distract them from being present. Neither bears the burden of the struggle to remain unseen.

We live in a world where to fit in we accept a need to present ourselves in a certain light. Thoughts and feelings about experiences that we all share are internally censored. Only those passing strict, appropriate inspection receive our approval to be expressed. And whatever the justification, be it political correctness, societal expectations, or psychological norms, we effectually cut ourselves off from the spontaneity of living, and the sublime joy of seeing ourselves in the eyes of a stranger.

Everyone enters and leaves this earth journey with nothing but our awareness of the great love and commonality we share. Between these two points we all rise, fall, triumph, break, fear, hope, laugh, cry, dream, blame, forgive and live the best that we are within a mystery that none of us really comprehends.

Why pretend that we don't share the same emptiness and the same desire to come together and fill it?

Right now I take
care of myself. I
listen, love and
accept the mystery
of my journey.
Where I am going
is beyond the
restraint of where
I have been.

REPOSE

"When it is dark enough, you can see the stars."

          ... *Ralph Waldo Emerson*

Today, I don't feel creative, wise, witty or even competent. There's a heaviness weighing me to the ground; a sorrow over having left so much behind, feeling that I'll never return, and not knowing where I'm going.

Time seems pressing upon me but without clear justification, like a bully on the back of the train shouting, *"You better get going. You better stay busy."* While the cars leave the station, I strain half-heartedly to hear his fading ranting.

"What's he saying!" I think it's supposed to be important, but I can't remember. Only a vague, memory remaining and a curiosity as to why my body feels such tenseness without obvious cause.

"No, wait," the voice is coming back. But it's different; the tone much softer, the delivery so gentle and clear. And I'm no longer sulking in the hollows of the station, but aware of new freedom and my heart's movement towards it.

"Be still, calm and wait. Nothing is required of you in this moment. Listen, watch, feel, sigh, laugh and cry. Settle back into the tenderness that supports you. I have Infinite Faith in you. Rest now and trust in the rhythm of the rails. This is a trip worth taking. Trust Me."

*I confidently greet
this day, because
what I carry
within me is more
than enough to
meet anything in
the moment that it
appears.*

CONFIDENCE IS JUSTIFIED

"Ya can't be no ghost. Ya gotta be a spirit."
            ... Jeremy Pikser & Warren Beatty, from the movie, Bulworth

When it's our turn to bat, there are a couple ways to approach it; holding back so we won't embarrass ourselves, or swinging for the fences.

In the former, we place ourselves at the mercy of who is pitching. Maybe if we don't swing, he will miss the strike zone and walk us.

Option two is quite different. We approach the plate with the assurance that whatever we do, we're going to make a difference. Yes, we might strike out, but we're also in position to drive in the winning run.

In true confidence, we don't need to resist fear, because that just sustains the drama. And if we force ourselves to push through it, what do we really achieve, but more attachment to our ability to betray ourselves, over prizes that fade away through time?

Self-assurance comes through the faith that we are always superior to circumstance. It frees us to be our greatness; taking away the strain of playing small.

As you stroll to the batters box or to any situation, relax. It's not nervousness that you are feeling, but the adrenaline of your brilliance. Step up, settle in and seize the moment. Whatever happens, it's going to raise the game. The crowd is on its feet.

*I am not as I
appear and neither
are you. I forgive
myself for missing
the wonder that
is coming out
of us through
such mysterious
expressions.*

LOST IN GRACE

"Rabbi Zusya said that on the Day of Judgment, God would ask him, not why he had not been Moses, but why he had not been Zusya."

... Walter Kaufmann

Authenticity is the heart of spiritual expression. It's how truth displays itself through the human soul. The term, however, is bantered around in spiritual circles and good intentioned society with little understanding of the depth of its meaning.

Oftentimes it's associated with being open and respectfully amendable to one's character flaws within a tolerable degree of self-containment. Although this appears to point to a delicious absolute, it is nothing more than mental exercise.

Authenticity is always leading us into ruthless self-honesty and it will not be contained by societal, psychological or personal expectations and norms.

Everyone, in fact, is always authentic. However we behave, from the seemingly most sublime to the most depraved, we are always expressing ourselves genuinely, as the person we believe ourselves to be, within the world that we believe we are in.

Authenticity is not a measure of our soul development or spiritual prowess. It is the open window into the truth of how we are experiencing ourselves and one another within the Mystery of awakening to our perfection.

It is how we give human expression to the pain, joy and confusion of mistaking ourselves for so much less than we are.

Illumination

ILLUMINATION

I left my hotel and walked until I came upon a gathering in a small urban park. It was my first time in Manhatten. The sounds, sights and smells of the big city mesmerized me.

The crowd was enthusiastically engaged with someone or something; eyes brightly open, wide smiles and joyous laughter. As I came closer a story began to unfold—a young preacher in a dark suit, white shirt and tie, with Bible in hand and his entourage behind him, seemed to be whipping up the crowd with his words.

But there was more. A white-faced mime, with reddened lips, a black and white striped interloper, sandwiched between the preacher and his crowd. His back was turned to the holy man while he performed.

"Give your heart to Jesus and you will be saved!" roared the evangelist. The mime, straight-faced with hands over his heart, mimicking the thumping of his heart, mocked the park padre's every word. And the crowd roared with raucous approval.

Frustration building in the preacher's voice, he pointed towards the mimic, bellowing even louder, more passionately his message, *"Beware of Satan and his minions!"* The mime responded, portraying horns, a tail and a nasty sneer.

The fastidious gathering suddenly turned stormy, jeering the speaker's aides as they attempted to escort the mime away. Quickly releasing him, the enforcers turned to query their leader. Hesitating, he waved them back, launching passionately, another barrage of rhetoric, with the mime countering his every thrust and parry.

Stepping back, I surveyed the whole scene. The backdrop of skyscrapers, the brilliance of the sunny day, a flight of birds overhead and above and behind the theater-in-the-park, a trio of homeless sojourners standing on a raised grassy knoll, paper bags in hand, tipping their wine and taking in the whole of the passion play below.

Suddenly the wonder of it all overwhelmed me. How surreal; the passion of those who would save, passing through the apathy of those engaged with the fool, mocking the righteous intention. And all the while, the three whose state appeared most open to these waves of pious intention, observed from behind this psychic battle, unseen and untouched by the invitation.

In that moment I saw perfection. The stage beautifully set, the daylight highlighting every detail, the script magnificently composed, every player fully immersed in character and flawlessly versed in their lines.

And the audience; me and the three wise men, caught up in the awe of the performance. Catching each others eyes, we spoke not a word, not even a gesture. If we were to laugh, we might cry.

Life seems to imitate art, however, it's the other way around. The Art of Living seen through Illumination (Full Lighting) gives us Clear Perspective as the Observer of It. Instead of losing ourselves in the storyline and the need to make sense of it all, that is, to craft our own version of *"the happy ending"*, we learn to trust following a plotline that takes us beyond the drama into its Underlying Reality. Light reveals Bliss. It gives us faith in where and how the Mystery is taking us.

*I am a sensual
being, living in an
exquisitely sensual
world. Precious is
my presence here
and glorious is
my opportunity to
take notice.*

EYES TO SEE

"I cannot say exactly what the mysterious change was. I saw no new thing, but I saw all the usual things in a miraculous new light—in what I believe is their true light. I saw for the first time how wildly beautiful and joyous, beyond any words of mine to describe, is the whole of life."

... *Margaret Prescott Montague*

Any place is heaven when I am present, just as it can be hell when I'm not. Hell is the emptiness I feel when I can't find me, when I'm lost, burrowed deep into some amorphous hidey hole, unaware of how I put myself there. It's the overriding apathy I can feel towards a familiar state of sensual stagnation.

When I show up in the moment it's magical. Walking through the mall is a sensory feast. Time folds in on itself. I watch a young boy and his mother walking almost in slow motion. The focus in his eyes, how she turns her head, the bounce of his step lifting his shoulders and the folding of her skirt is rapturous. All sound, movement and sense is orchestral—perfectly measured.

I move towards the stairway and reaching for the wooden handrail I pause. I'm enamored with its form. *"How could I ever have missed this?"* I reach towards it slowly, softly, like a lover, anticipating the touch of the beloved's skin. Breathtaking. My fingers trail lightly, deliberately along its curves—the descent now serving my exploration.

It's so wondrously delicious when I'm truly here and have nowhere I need to go.

*I am a Divine
Masterpiece; the
perfectly thrown
pot, blemished
by the Master to
remind me of Her
love for my frailty,
Her joy in my
humility.*

SCARRED FOR LIGHT

"Real isn't how you are made, Said the Skin-Horse. It's a thing that happens to you ... by the time you are REAL, most of your hair has been loved off, and your eyes drop out, and you get loose in the joints and very shabby. But these things don't matter at all, because once you are REAL you can't be ugly, except to people who don't understand."

... Margery Williams, The Velveteen Rabbit

Walking into Taco Bell, I saw her from the side. Sixteen or so, young, dark, pretty, taking orders at the counter. The beauty of youthful innocence can be intoxicating.

As she turned to take my order my mind froze, the deep, ragged scar emblazoned down the length of her cheek had been hidden from me. *"It shouldn't be."* I argued, feeling shock to anger to empathy.

She just kept smiling. Teasing her co-worker, she turned to me with sparkling eyes, laughter lingering across her cheeks. *"May I take your order, sir?"* she beamed. I smiled too.

I sat with my lunch, unable to break my gaze on her. She never missed a beat. The joy in her presence was infectious and I had caught it. I couldn't see her imperfection anymore; the light of her countenance had blinded me to it.

That was many years ago and the memory of her still gratefully lingers.

I wonder. Would I have noticed the heavenliness of this fast food angel had her stigmata not drawn me near?

Perhaps the scars that we bear are the Universe's way of reminding us, how deep runs our beauty, how radiant our light.

*I forgive myself
for judging me.
I remember that
I was born to
express without
expectation and
that my actions
reflect not who I
am, but how love
has found its way
out through me.*

FORGETFUL TO A FAULT

"Do not say things. What you are stands over you the while, and thunders so that I cannot hear what you say to the contrary."

... Ralph Waldo Emerson

Years ago I read of a South African tribe's unique way of meeting the aberrant, antisocial behavior of one of its members.

The whole tribe would immediately stop what they were doing and gather in a ritual circle. Placing the offender in the center under a charge of silence, they proceeded to share publicly all of the kind, respectful and loving acts any and everyone could recall the accused ever having performed. The ritual would go for days until all memorable incidents were shared. Afterwards a celebration was held with the former transgressor where he was symbolically and officially welcomed back into the tribe.

Can you imagine a world with such intention for validating a confused or lost soul's choices? Or what kind of person each of us would be if we treated ourselves this way?

Instead of judging, criticizing or punishing ourselves for not living up to an expectation, we could instead, take the time to recall all of the compassionate, forgiving and selfless stands that we have taken?

We would begin to see how harshly we have judged ourselves and we would realize too, what failure really is; an opportunity to reclaim our nature and be welcomed back into the Grace of Being human again.

*My life is
a thrilling
adventure. Every
rise, drop, curve
and straight-a-
way carries me
into the discovery
of life and the joy
of trusting how I
live it.*

RAISE YOUR ARMS & SCREAM

"Security is mostly a superstition. It does not exist in nature. ... Life is either a daring adventure or nothing."

... Helen Keller

Life is the most thrilling roller coaster ride ever. The next span of track isn't even laid until the exact moment we get to it. To the logical mind this is madness, until immediacy reveals the perfect dance of resources and need.

When we first came to earth and the Whole Ride began we accepted that tracks of our life would run along many courses we'd be unfamiliar with. Still we had faith enough to climb on board, strap in and let go. Oftentimes we felt that we'd missed a turn and were lost, only to realize along the way that we'd never left the rails.

We discovered in us the power to choose how we experienced the ride we were living. At first, weighing heavily our decisions, worrying compulsively as to our destination, striving hard to correct our course, and attaching to the scenery to meet our future needs.

Then later, through the wisdom of experience, accepting what shows up to meet us, trusting beyond the blurred view of what we see, and giving into the sensations along the way.

And when the ride is over and the safety bar rises, we step off with a longing to get back on and do it all over again.

*I am a natural
performer. My
mind is at rest. I
am available for
life. I watch how
perfectly I express
what I am called
upon to do in the
act of doing it.*

IN THE ZONE

"Thinking is overrated!"
*... Jon Kitna, Seattle Seahawks Quarterback, in response to a reporter's question
about his outstanding performance, "What were you thinking at the time?"*

In May of 1987 the Los Angeles Lakers basketball team played the
Golden State Warriors in an NBA playoff series. The Lakers, featuring
future Hall-of-Famers Kareem Abdul-Jabbar and Magic Johnson were
highly favored and easily won the first three games. But in the fourth
game the Warriors rallied to win behind the spectacular play of Eric
"Sleepy" Floyd, who was virtually unstoppable.

Floyd hit almost every shot he took from awkward to near impossible
angles. When interviewed after the game, he told reporters that he was
in the zone and that the basket looked as big as a garbage can.

What's the zone? It's the place where Presence is and thinking isn't,
where activity is unhindered by consideration or choice. It's a function
of flow where Being expresses perfectly through spontaneous doing.

We, like professional athletes, can enter into this zone of awareness.
Sometimes it just happens. The veils of busyness part and there we
are, witnesses to life unfolding flawlessly, our every act and intention
harmoniously congruent.

Wisdom tells us that the zone is not the exception but the rule. And
like all experiences, the more we notice it the more opportunities we
have to live in it.

Letting Go

LETTING GO

He had been born into crawling. Everyone around him; his family and friends, teachers and peers, all got around that way. Even celebrities; the famous ones who seemed to have everything, told stories of their uphill climbs.

Lately though, the effort it was taking to keep on keeping on seemed monumental. And for what? More of the same? He was scaring himself with the thoughts he was thinking. *"What's the point of it all? What is everyone working for? Just to exist? Comfortably? Luxuriously? Basically?"*

He had lived all his life with a vision of something more, a true freedom of body, mind and heart. But with his every step forward, it seemed that his destination kept pace, moving that much further away.

"You could let it all go." the voice within him cried. *"Give up the climb and follow where life takes you."* *"Oh, but how could I do that?"* he lamented. *"I wouldn't know how."*

So on he crept, trying his best to push through his failing distractions, dissolving motivation and ineffective medications. He pushed himself mercilessly onward towards a fickle, unreasonable future, insanely resisting his heart's leading. Until … he could go no further.

In that moment he stopped, facing the futility of fighting himself. He paused instead just to breathe. And the questions came clearly to him.

"Could there be more to me, and to my life, than crawling towards what I think I want and need? Can I be certain that this is all there is to me?"

"Yes, I could be mistaken!"

"And if so, what have I lost, and what am I now losing, by continuing to force myself to live this way?"

"Everything! All my hopes and dreams of discovering myself and the world I am curious about." he realized.

"What would my life look like and how would I feel if I was just about following my wonder right now? Trusting in this moment's leading of it?"

"I wouldn't be crawling towards what I hate. I would be sailing with the wind, alive, excited, unsure and loving it?"

"But I don't know how!" his certainty shot back, ready to reassume his laborious position.

"But then again," he smiled, *"do I really know I have to know that?"*

Suddenly, the world opened up before him. The generic nagging in his mind dropped away. The flowers across the street leaped into view, as he noticed his desire to give them to her.

Blissfully, he flew across the street.

Letting go is your soul breathing out. You do so when you are finished taking in whatever it is that has captured you. You may need to wrestle with what you're holding within until you are fully intimate with its essence. From relationships to behaviors, it can take years of time or a single moment for you to *get* what you seek in it. It is exactly then, that you breathe it out and let it go—no sooner, no later. Letting go is not something you do. It happens when you quit trying.

*I now sense the
present power and
life in my body,
my being, my
thinking and my
world. I notice
too, how harsh
it feels holding
onto a future that
I must pretend
someday might be.*

K.I.S.S.

"But I marvel at how this great wealth has made its home in this poverty."
... Jesus the Christ, The Gospel According to Thomas

Spirituality is no big deal. It's as natural as rain falling. What's complex is our thinking about it.

It's simple to turn within and know the peace that passes all understanding, but it requires us to let go of the compulsive need to understand it. Here, we can't have our cake and eat it too, for tasking our minds to comprehend the incomprehensible is exactly what keeps us occupied and unavailable for experiencing this mystery.

Sensing our body and surroundings turns off the thinking mode of our minds giving us immediate access to peace of mind. By noticing the sensations in our body or the busyness of our experience, we become present with what is happening and with ourselves as well. Joyous realization of the union of observer and the observed expands and sharpens awareness.

All we need do to break off this love affair with life's immediacy, is to stop noticing it by starting to think about it again.

It's really no big deal though. Why not notice how painful it feels to be compulsively avoiding a circumstance you might be worry free of, if you had faith in your ability to face it? It's a great start.

*I let go and accept
this moment. I
know that it now
provides perfectly
for me and that it
will continue to do
so whenever I am
in it.*

Turn Loose

"A man there was and they called him mad;
The more he gave, the more he had."

... *John Bunyan*

We have two operating intentions: holding back or letting go. Attempting to control the flow of circumstance results in stagnation, pressure and suffering. It's like pinching off a garden hose for fear that the flow of water might cease. Believing that by doing so we'd at least have the water that's backed up in it.

But the flow of life substance is irresistible and waits upon no one's expectations. Whatever is hoarded, be it money, ideas or relationships, degrades from lack of use into energy draining piles of trivial attachments that block our access to what can be.

Pressure as well, builds from resistance to flow and eventually our hands and hearts tire from the effort it takes to suppress it. And all the while we're oblivious to this same current that richly expresses through unrestrained channels.

Relief is so simple. Just let go of what we're holding onto—trusting in this moment's supply to keep showing up with whatever it is that we need.

Release is actually the only course possible. Like holding our breath, when we assume we can continue our withholding intention, our body soon shows us just how unequivocally mistaken we are.

The realization of my highest good is a gift already given. I wait patiently in the moment for its arrival.

CLEARED FOR LANDING

"Temptation is the desire to settle for less than the best. Don't let the good get in the way of the best."

… Nikos Kazant

Much of the stress we suffer in the world comes not through our apparent failures, but in our seeming successes. In achieving that which we think is good for us we often attach to less than what our souls long for.

Now, a two-fold problem appears—how to recognize and experience what is truly in our hearts, as well as how to release our connection with what seems less than fulfilling.

Relationships with loved ones, friends, work and other activities can easily become frozen in the suffering of repeated attempts to make better choices or to escape from poor ones.

The solution lies not in better analysis of the situation or increased effort toward making changes. That can only bring us more of the same. Take the radically different tact of *letting go and giving it a rest.*

It's only our frantic circling above the runway of our minds that keeps the arrival of our highest intentions in a holding pattern. When we get out of the way air traffic starts to flow again.

Patience doesn't take up our time. It removes it as a barrier to immediate experience.

*I notice and listen
to my pain. It
shows me where I
don't need to hurt.
In fact, it's one of
my best friends.*

CLEAN & SOBERING

"How can the angels sleep when the devil leaves the porch light on?"
... Tom Waits

Compulsive behavior warrants our respect and close inquiry. To treat it with anything less insures harsh, painful experience that only forces us to repeat once again, treating it with respect and close inquiry. There's no getting around this.

Prayer and meditation help us surrender our experience. In the light of this awareness, the insanity of living false beliefs is exposed and consequently collapses.

Prayer and affirmation, however, are often used in desperation as clever guises to avoid honest inquiry into the lies we've accepted. To affirm the truth of our Being without acknowledging the enslavement we've suffered for our adulterated beliefs and their subservient thoughts, is to deny the Light within us; the Power that can reveal and release us from them.

We can pray and affirm till the cows come home that we're loved and supported by Spirit. Yet until we're willing to know and accept how innocently, mistakenly and yet willfully we defend those beliefs that oppose these truths, we remain imprisoned by them.

Grace is interminable. It presses relentlessly against the pain threshold of our self-deceit. Why test the limits of suffering simply to discover there's no need for it?

I am now free
from all that has
been. I embrace
this moment,
grateful for it's
leading me into
the freshness of
what can be.

BREAKTHROUGH

"And the day came when the risk it took to remain in a bud was more painful than the risk it took to blossom."

… Anais Nin

Change can feel unsettling. There are those moments within discovery when the ground of reason falls in upon uncertainty. And the fear of letting go even into glories unknown can keep us absurdly bound to painfully familiar circumstance.

Can you imagine what nature would be like if animals worried like humans. Birds would stop flying, for what mother would risk pushing her baby out into the sky. Caterpillars would medicate their butterfly urgings and salmon cease to struggle upstream—life everywhere would stop to weigh the fear of uncertainty in order to abort or modify the effort.

Fortunately life is resolute and no respecter of human will. Interwoven within all parts are the threads of evolution that not only connect us, but draw us collectively through mystery into new awareness and acceptance, regardless of how we manipulate our experience of it.

Resistance forces pain, and pain forces the release of what's resisted. Eventually we begin to see the painful futility of holding on to what we suffer for, as well as the infinite web of joy and freedom that's poised to catch and release us the moment we fall into it.

Breathe deep. You're learning to let go.

Peace

PEACE

In the classic movie, "City Slickers" Curly, the intimidating trail boss, delivers a shot of advice, punctuated with a potent one-liner to Mitch, a wannabe cowboy.

"You city people have everything all mixed up. You spend all your time burning the candle at both ends, burning up your lives minute by minute. And then you get your guts all full of knots and ulcers and heart problems and you come out here expecting me to help you unravel everything for you."

And then he holds up one finger, the index finger and says: *"You don't have the sense to realize that life is all about one thing and one thing only."*

And then he stops talking.

Mitch, frustrated by Curly's silence, finally breaks it with the obvious.

"Okay, okay Curly. I give up. Life is about one thing. What is that one thing?"

Curly takes a puff on his hand rolled cigarette, looks him straight in the eye and says, *"That's for you to figure out."*

It still is for us to figure out what life is all about. In getting worn down through the living of it, we can't get away from the simple desire for lasting peace of mind.

My teacher punctuated the truth of this by modeling it through one of the most horrific experiences we can imagine; the murder of His innocence.

To see His willingness to surrender His life, to die on a cross as some sort of ransom or enlightened act of Divine Will, is to miss completely the essence of His living it.

He had found the one thing that Curly was pointing to, the one thing that made total sense out of life, that brought Him full, lasting peace. He had discovered that no matter what circumstance is facing Him, He was always superior to it—no exceptions. He was free from having to expend any of His life energy by making up stories about what was happening and what He should do about it. He let nothing take Him away from the Glory of living His life.

He knew that whatever life presented, he could not only face it, He could appreciate and have faith in it showing up as a blissful experience.

He was a man completely at peace with Himself in a safe, beautiful world.

Peace is not what happens around you. It's what happens inside you. It has no correlation with the stories of what is going on in you or your world. It's the solid foundation you stand on, where you can view the wonder of you happening.

When you realize this, the world can finally be what it was always intended to be—a paradise. A place where every one, every thing and every circumstance does *just one thing*; shows you how wondrously, mysteriously and securely connected you are in it. Peace of mind establishes the earth as your playground, giving you the freedom, encouragement and safety net to try out all of the equipment.

*There is nothing
more important
than the quiet
time I take for me.
I am grateful for
these delicious bites
of Being.*

JOY OF BEING

"There is no pleasure comparable to not being captivated by any external thing whatsoever."

... *Thomas Wilson*

By identifying ourselves with our minds we unconsciously forsake our ability to form clear intention by falling into the fuzziness of compulsive thinking and nonstop busyness.

How does this play out? At first and perhaps for many years, it seems comfortable or reasonably interesting, a way to stay distracted from the pain of neglecting honest self-inquiry, losing ourselves in the many bells and whistles around us. At some point, though, it begins to dawn on us that even our new toys have no luster and that compulsive doing has become wearisome. We yearn for something that is simpler and more satisfying

Being still and present can seem uncomfortable at first, because of the mind's insistence upon staying occupied. But in giving ourselves to the moment, we discover that rather than pleasantly distracting us, it frees and fulfills us. We are home once again, basking in the glorious experience of sensing, breathing and being, reveling in the knowing that is our Divine Inheritance.

Feel the wind, smell the sea, touch your coffee cup, and sigh. Give your spirit a chance to catch up with you.

*I am ageless. I am
younger and more
vibrant today than
I have ever been.
I bathe my cells in
the promise of my
being and the love
of its expression.*

BODY LANGUAGE

"Everyone is the age of their heart."

... *Guatemalan Proverb*

Age isn't visible in years, but in vibrancy. When our bodies are alive with vitality our eyes glow, our hair glistens, our whole form radiates. Whether we're seventeen or seventy, liveliness attracts and transforms.

Science has shown that our bodies respond not to biological mandate, but to what we believe and how our thoughts instruct the cells.

This is freeing to know, for presently our sense of identity is going through a major shift from *who we ought to be* to *who we have always been*. One of the early signs is a change in our use of our life force. The energy we previously used for *making our lives better* is lessening while at the same time we're discovering increasing reserves of faith and support for letting the perfection of our natural selves show up spontaneously.

Depression, frustration and hopelessness are valid expressions of our failing ability to hold on to what was; a natural response to our surrender into the uncertainty of who we can be. Wisely we recognize that even though our bodies may suffer through these changes, we don't have to identify this transition with stories about the ravages of aging.

Believe in the life that is your body. It will renew itself to match the vitality of your spirit.

I am held safe in
the Heart of Life.
I exist to witness
how the gift of my
life has meaning.
I rely upon the
Grace that has
created me, to
show me this.

TIME TO COME HOME

"It takes so much to be a full human being . . . One has to abandon altogether the search for security and reach out to the risk of living with both arms. One has to embrace the world like a lover, and yet demand no easy return of love."

...Morris West

As infants we had no difficulty trusting the universe. We knew no other way. Our entrance into the world necessitated reliance upon the kindness and assistance from others.

Whenever one door closed, another always opened and even though our experience under another's care may have seemed slight, peppered with confusion or pleasantly substantial, it materialized none-the-less.

It's easy to forget that we came into this existence with nothing. Everything we now have, including the abilities we use to cope in this world, were shown to us through our experiences of meeting mystery within circumstance. This would be wise to remember, for none of us can truly stand on our seeming accomplishments separate from those who've helped us along the way.

And still we remain highly dependent. For who can claim to regulate their heartbeat and blood flow, maintain the planet's precise distance from the sun, or control the forces that bring us into the world and eventually takes us from it.

We're still nursing at the Universe's breast. We have just disguised the cry of our hunger. *"I think I hear my Mother (Universe) calling?"*

I am here now.
So is everything
I could want
or need. My
greatest blessing
and deepest joy is
standing right in
front of me.

SOUND OF SILENCE

"Among the great things which are to be found among us, the Being of Nothingness is the greatest."

... Leonardo da Vinci

Nothing compares with the joy of being.

In this present moment we are released from the past: how we have suffered for our beliefs misplacing our sense of purpose, accruing dues and regrets that were never ours to repay. Suddenly, none of this has any significance when yesterday has no claim upon today.

In the Now there can be no anxiety about the future: who we might or might not become, the consequences of better or worse choices, feared or anticipated outcomes, chance or fate. For whether our concern is an instant or decade away, without thought of tomorrow, the threat of its content is null and void.

In this present moment there is nothing to become, no missing pieces to be found. Feelings are available to be purely experienced without the stories that twist and distort what we need to do with them and thoughts await our conscious intention to think them. In the now, the world unfolds without difficulty, all life has immeasurable meaning, silence collapses space limitations, stillness dissolves time into eternity and everything that is before us shines within the light of its creation.

Nothing compares with the joy of being.

*I am peace and
I enjoy serenity.
Life presents itself
for my simple
discovery and joy.
I have no need to
make problems or
stress out of it.*

SKIP TO THE ENDING

"Any fool can make a rule, and every fool will mind it."

... *Henry David Thoreau*

As a child I'd get into trouble sometimes by following a playmate's lead. When my mother questioned me, I'd give her the excuse that, "he did it, so I thought I could too." My mom's stock reply was always, "If he jumped off a cliff, would you do that too?"

It's a childhood lesson that can take a lifetime to learn.

Take stress for instance. It's generally believed that it's unavoidable and that a little of it actually helps us to achieve. Many of our role models emerge in stories of their heroic struggles through stress and the drama's that cause tension.

But is stress; our reaction to expectation, really necessary?

When we resist the reality of what is, we form tension within ourselves by our choice to oppose, overcome or fall victim to what we've decided reality looks like. It's high drama and loaded with stress.

It goes like this. We're well. We see reality, make it a problem and get stressed over it. We overcome the problem and we're well again.

Why not skip the middleman and just stay well? But if you really want stress, it's OK. Make up a problem and knock yourself out.

Possibilities

POSSIBILITIES

A friend called me the other day, desperate from the situation that was facing him. The woman he loved had told him that she didn't want to see him anymore.

"I don't know what to do, Dale. I'm afraid I'm not going to make it. I feel so much pain. The last time I felt like this I tried to kill myself and I'm afraid I might go there again. I feel so lost, so lonely, so worthless."

After hearing him out, he asked me for help. With no rational solution in mind, I spoke clearly to him, quite amazed with the authority that I was speaking to him with.

"Mark, I need you to really listen to me. Can you do that?"

He agreed.

"There is nothing wrong with you. It's just your mind torturing you. I only have ten minutes, because I need to be with someone very shortly, but we won't need much time."

"For me to help you, I need you to follow my instructions. Will you do this? And I won't ask you to do anything that you can't or that is harmful."

"I'll try my best." He ached back at me.

"Good, that will be more than enough." I assured him.

"Right now, I need you to give me three possibilities for how Sharon leaving you might be the best thing that she could ever do for you."

"I can't do that Dale. I can't make it without her."

"Mark, we only have eight minutes left. You can do this. I'm not saying you have to let her go. All I am asking of you is to give me three scenarios for how her leaving could work for you."

He weighed what I was asking of him. I waited … I waited longer … and finally he spoke.

"Well, I guess if she's not the right person for me, it would be better if she wasn't with me?"

"Good." I said. *"Now give me another."*

He struggled courageously, *"iiiff ... someone better for me were to show up, I would be available to be with her."*

"You're doing great Mark, one more."

He gave me more than three possibilities and with each consideration, I could hear his voice lifting and his spirit coming back to life.

"Wow, Dale. I never thought of this. Sharon leaving, might really be the best thing that ever happened to me."

"That could be true, Mark, very true."

He finished with a couple minutes to spare.

In every situation your world is resplendent with ripe possibilities. It's only your clinging to familiar outcomes that keeps you from seeing them. If you want to see what is possible in your life, try making friends with the undesirable circumstance that you are resisting. You will discover that like a magician, it has many more wonders up its sleeve than you could ever imagine. Possibilities love to present themselves to an appreciative audience.

*I wait to see how I
am used to express
reality rather than
busying myself
with how to make
a better illusion.*

PULL OVER & TURN
OFF YOUR ENGINE

"It is easier to fight for one's principles than to live up to them."

... Alfred Adler

One of the ego's knocks on Being Present is that it's passive. *"What would ever get done in this world if we just sat around doing nothing?"* it barks.

Well, yes. We'd have no wars, murders, violence, incivility, abuse or other unconscious actions, if we weren't about doing them.

There'd be fewer suicides, depression, addiction and mental disease without the stress of incessant competition and the irrational compulsion to keep busy.

Heartache, isolation, loneliness and the grief of separation would decrease if we couldn't justify our compulsive doing as the reason for neglecting to give ourselves and those we love, the attention of our interest.

So yes, a lot of what gets done to avoid enjoying a better world just wouldn't happen.

Silly? Perhaps ... to the mind broker that would corral in the idea of where life ought to venture rather than risk jumping on its back and riding off into the experience of it.

Being Present is far from passive. It takes passionate desire to discover how activity can serve to fulfill, instead of dampen, and a daring spirit willing to follow what's revealed. When it comes to doing something, it might be wise to consider if it's an improvement on doing nothing.

*I am grateful for
this opportunity
to know you, for
our willingness to
let each other in
and for our faith
in shared discovery
along the journey.*

THE SOUL LESS TRAVELED

"If we only love those who appear whole and well, then who will love us?"
... Dale Blackford

One of my great joys is exploring roads off the beaten path. When new to an area I get to know my way around by learning the main travel routes, but it's the smaller, less traveled ones that I find most charming.

Streams, lakes, mountains and canyons lie tucked away within an interior where often, only small country roads, winding curves and one-lane bridges lead. Regularly the least promising path provides the richest access to wonders that few travelers ever see.

People are a lot like this too. We can assess others by taking the familiar communication routes that are well traveled. How a person appears, thinks and reacts, i.e. the broad, linear personality traits that their words, opinions and intentions portray, tell us little more than how to navigate comfortably around them.

What if I turned off of your main highway and onto the unmarked road you've left open? That way might be rocky, poorly maintained, and it could narrow or end. I'll have to watch for sharp curves, occasionally stop and ask for directions and get used to not knowing where I am going.

But it's worth the uncertainty. What treasures wait inside you that I might be the first to see?

I now surrender
the loneliness
of striving to fit
in, for the joy of
awakening to the
community that
knows me.

EXPLORE NEW WORLDS

"I always prefer to believe the best of everybody, it saves so much trouble."
... Rudyard Kipling

What if we live in a world where mystery is the norm? A place where we realize that everyone is groping equally within a context far greater than our capacity to understand it?

What if we accept that to comprehend anything in our world, we need everything each one of us has to offer; our diverse perspective of what is before us, our unique belief of its meaning, and our personal calling for expressing it. Like a puzzle, with the filling in of each vital piece, what appears before us, blindly fragmented and insignificant, suddenly begins to clarify; taking cohesive, transcendent shape.

What if what we long for is far too grand and sweet for one soul to entertain, yet perfectly fit for expressing through all of us together? What if we trust one another to faithfully fulfill our role in this collective unfolding, because we have soul evidence that there is no other course possible?

What if we can see all individual struggle and strife as a necessary part of awakening to the awareness of this fluid Reality. And that we know that the losses of what we, alone, fight so hard to hold on to, are worth the sacrifices we now make together, to be joyous and free.

Today I surrender
to my vision. I
allow my Spirit
to give birth to
it, trusting that I
have within me,
and all around
me, all that is
needed to let it
grow.

BODACIOUS VISION

"Far away there in the sunshine are my highest aspirations. I may not reach them, but I can look up and see their beauty, believe in them, and try to follow where they lead."

... Louisa May Alcott

Visions are transforming. They offer views into possibilities that can be universally expansive and inclusively ideal. Clear vision entices others to enlist in it, drawing out the best in them and mobilizing resources towards its realization.

Life affirming visions are especially powerful as they celebrate Divine Intention. They are in tune with a Rhythm that richly expresses their purpose and an order of sequence for fulfilling them.

Envisioning requires no rationalizing in the process. It pushes the envelope far beyond the limits of human understanding; tapping collective resources that are linked with global evolution, cooperation and harmony.

Our visions lead us on a journey beyond the most awe-inspiring results, through the most imaginative vehicles we might ever consider. They offer us opportunities to witness the beauty, joy, and wonder of our Being, in concert with all the people, ideas, and life experiences that vision attracts and employs for its purpose.

You needn't be afraid of great dreams—in fact, the bigger the better. Visions so grand, so magnificent, that they require legions of angels to accomplish, insure that you can't get in the way. And if you are not in the way, you're in the flow.

*I am sailing with
friends upon
peaceful, forgiving
waters. My heart
is already in
Paradise. My
course has been set
to experience it.*

PARADISE

"One does not discover new lands without consenting to lose sight of the shore for a very long time."

... *André Gide*

Can you imagine those brave islanders who launched out in tiny crafts, sailing thousands of miles across uncharted seas to discover Hawaii? They had no forerunners, no maps, no clue as to their destination, yet from unfathomable uncertainty, they landed on pristine, welcoming shores.

They were people like you and me; following their hearts, trusting in their guidance, believing they would be led along the way. Their faith was necessary, having accepted the loss of a familiar existence that no longer served them.

How must they have felt as they watched their homeland dissolve into the vastness of the sea; confining them to the floor boards of their vessels.

Yes, they found paradise, but in truth, they did so long before setting foot ashore. They discovered that by releasing the known in favor of the unseen, the joy and wonder of new possibilities became evident.

What's been familiar for you that's now slipping beneath the waves? Ask yourself, *"If I could, would I go back? What was the cost of my staying and the possible gain for my releasing it?"* Turn to the horizon with your fellow castaways. We've set sail together for paradise.

Presence

PRESENCE

As a young boy my grandfather taught me the meaning of Presence. He lived it. Arguably a religious man, Grampa was a devout Baptist who, as a deacon, led prayers and other church functions.

I knew very little about this part of him. He lived in Omaha, Nebraska, fifty miles from my home in Lincoln. I only saw him in his church once my whole life.

But he was my spiritual mentor, practicing the heart of his faith through his gentle attentiveness and enthusiastic appreciation of wonder. Whenever Grampa would come over to our house, he would come up to me when no one else was looking, he'd lean down and whisper to me, *"Dale"*. And with a twinkle in his eye and a turn of his head, I knew that he had something just for me to hear, usually a unique and funny story.

On one such visit he took me aside and began this tale.

A man walked into a bar with no money and wanted a drink. The bartender wouldn't give him one, so he tried to strike a bargain.

"Look," the man said, *"If I show you something you have never, ever seen before, will you give me a drink?"*

"Okay," Said the bartender, *"but it had better be worth it or I'm throwing you out afterwards."*

The man reached in his coat pocket and pulled out a tiny piano and a tiny piano bench. After setting them on the counter, he reached in another pocket and pulled out a little mouse in a tuxedo, and setting him on the bench in front of the piano, the mouse began to play.

The bartender, dumbfounded, could hardly speak. As he poured the man a tall beer, he blurted out *"That is the most incredible thing I have ever seen!"*

"There's more." Said the man. *"If it's even better can I have as many drinks as I want?"*

"Anything!" agreed the bartender.

The man then reached into his pocket and pulled out a yellow canary in a black, strapless dress, set her on the piano and she began to sing to the mouse's accompaniment.

"That's it!" exclaimed the bartender. *"You have to sell me those two. I will give you anything you want, even this bar. Name your price!"*

The man hesitated apologetically begging, *"No, no, I really couldn't."*

But the bartender insisted. He would not take no for an answer, plying the man with everything he could think of.

Finally, the man said, *"Sir, I would sell them to you, only, I would be cheating you."*

"What?" said the barkeep.

"Well, that canary can't really sing."

"No? What do you mean?"

"Well, you see … that mouse … he's a ventriloquist."

Your Presence is the only real gift you can give to another, the only one that is lasting. When you show up as who you are, without mask or intention, simply for the experience of sharing the moment with another, you enrich more than just two lives, you bless the world.

The story of how Spirit has formed itself as you discloses itself through your Presence. It helps everyone see how the same Spirit is unfolding as their story as well. Presence harmonizes all our differences, crosses through all our barriers and brings everyone and everything together.

*This is the first
moment of the rest
of my life. I would
rather experience
it than think
about it.*

Came To Believe

"Every decision is like a murder and our march forward is over the stillborn bodies of all our possible selves that will never be."

... *Rene Dubos*

Alcohol, food, and sex can be addictive when used to mask feelings and avoid situations that stimulate them. What defines an *addict* is not the use of these things but the inner compulsion that drives their usage.

If we accept compulsivity as the standard for addiction, a whole world of medicating practice emerges, from relationships to religion to any and every form of distraction.

So, consider our obsession with having to make the right decision—about anything—and the compulsive thinking we do about it. For most, this is the drug of choice that keeps us unavailable to the immediate experience of living, and numb to the pain, anger and sorrow of doing so.

The condition is exacerbated by a society that affirms our addiction as appropriate use of thought and validates the control junkie's urging: *"Look, if you don't make the right choice, you'll suffer for it. So before you decide, think it over, hard and long."*

We suffer because we're *using* compulsive appraising to avoid present moment accepting. Are we certain a decision is required? Is it possible the matter could take care of itself? What could be possible if our thinking did not keep us distracted from the experience?

Restore us to sanity?

*I take the step
that's before me,
knowing that the
Universe will show
me the next one.*

No Decision

"... as a man's real power grows and his knowledge widens, ever the way he can follow grows narrower: until at last he chooses nothing, but does only and wholly what he must do."

... *Ursula K. Le Guin*

So much of our time and life energy can be spent on contemplating a right or wrong choice—thinking that by making an error we'll set into motion an undesirable and unalterable course of events. Without a conscious examination of our irrational worries, the act of decision-making can blow up into such a monster, that only indecision seems possible—our thoughts frozen solid in confusion.

First of all, relax. There is no right or wrong choice, only different ways of exploring a Universe that fully supports our education in so doing. Choice is simply a mental exercise, a broad, forgiving way for us to experiment with human desire as we learn about how inconceivably perfect the Divine Intention is within us and how it naturally finds Its own way of expression.

As we become present through trial, error, inspiration and ultimately release, we notice that there is a full, expansive flow to life and that we're always attune with its enfoldment. Confidence and the joy of our Being dissolves away all fear and trepidation about what to do. The way before us instantly reveals itself in the very moment we release ourselves from compulsively seeking it.

*I walk moment
by moment in the
direction of my
dreams, confident
of Spirit's leading
through all
appearances.*

STRAIGHT FORWARD

"The best way out is always through."

... *Robert Frost*

When we fix our minds upon a specific plan, object or experience, we not only limit the potential of our journey, we miss the view along the way.

Our thinking relies upon past memories as a way of mapping projected strategies to avoid any confusing, frightening or other seemingly unpleasant outcomes. This is our mind's attempt to replicate experiences of relief from previously threatening appearances, and to reassure us with the notion that resistance to a reappearing set of circumstances is noble work.

This is a story that never ends, until we stop validating our retelling of it through our thinking and actions.

Life is a rich, full adventure, not a problem-solving set of tasks. Mystery may appear foreboding, but it gently reveals itself as we enter into it rather than skirting the familiar route around it.

Follow the road where it leads, not where you remember it has taken you.

*I wait for the
meaning this
present experience
has to show me. I
use this moment
to take notice of
all that is within,
before and around
me.*

LISTEN FOR THE SINGING

"There are joys which long to be ours. God sends ten thousand truths, which come about us like birds seeking inlet; but we are shut up to them, and so they bring us nothing, but sit and sing awhile upon the roof, and then fly away."

... Henry Ward Beecher

When considering the situations we appear to attract into our lives it's wise to do so lightly. For although it's true that we experience what we hold in mind, looking to change circumstance by tracing it back to how we thought it into existence will do little but build frustration.

Our minds work best when we let go of our critical thinking and allow spirit to channel new information, inspiration and guidance.

The law of cause and effect, which is relative to earthly form, insures that the clarity of our thinking determines how effective we are in manifesting what we focus on. However, when our experience transcends the personal, the Principle of Unified Grace applies, where nothing that happens on earth is made better or worse by our thinking.

We begin to see how everything from disease and disaster to breakthroughs and miracles is constantly serving up immediate opportunities for our greater understanding and freedom. Our attitude shifts to anticipate how Life will expand our experience beyond the certainties of our judgments.

In the world of matter every situation is critically affected by how we think about it. In Spirit none of this matters because every situation has a precious and vital gift to impart to us.

*My life is far
richer; more
possible than I
can imagine or
conceive. I show
up in the moment
to participate in it.*

ONCE UPON A TIME

"Sell your cleverness and buy bewilderment."

... *Jalal ud-Din Rumi*

To be sure of anything in the world is to reduce it to its most familiar elements, relationships and perspectives. Predictability then seems possible because of the narrow view that's taken. Those who become adept at manipulating this myopia are perceived as being clever, even successful.

Yet who is richer, wiser and more free, the king of the fishbowl or the beggar who wanders the seas?

We may think we can *will* our world by shrinking it within the confines of our understanding, but in truth we only exclude ourselves moment by moment from heaven.

The drain upon our life energy in sustaining this exclusion is immense. Pain, fear and suffering build up under the chronic pressure to conform. Eventually we become weary of the burden—tiring of our pride ever denying our hunger and loneliness.

The way of fulfillment is not complex, just reversed. We have to trust in what we don't know and can't control. It's within the seeming tenuousness of the moment that its Divine Potency is revealed—where our natural genius and life's utter simplicities emerge.

A queen confined or a maiden free. Who really lives happily every moment?

Self-Love

SELF-LOVE

I could see the light at the end of the tunnel and it felt exciting. I had been working on this book for two years and needed to write just a few more pages to complete and publish it.

But the last few pages were not coming easily and I had given myself an uncharacteristic deadline to complete them. So with a sense of duty I sat down in my favorite coffee shop (my second office), plugged in my computer, and prepared to write.

"You can't get that model anymore. Thirteen inch is the smallest screen Apple makes now." he spoke, unsolicited, gesturing towards my machine.

Looking up, I answered, *"Yea. I really like it. This baby's lasted me almost six years. I told myself I'd get a new one when I finished my book."*

"So, you're a writer" he continued. Straining through his British-like accent and the noise of the coffee shop, I leaned forward to better hear him.

Expecting him to soon drop our chat and return to his open computer, I listened attentively until, after several minutes, I began to realize that he was moving beyond a casual discourse.

In my mind I could hear *that voice* consulting me, *"You need to find a way to end this politely, so you can get busy with what you came here to do. You have work to do."*

"... it's a different world in New Zealand." He went on. *"People drive cars thirty years and older and think nothing of it. They don't waste anything. My first car was an old Hudson. Remember them? My dad rebored the engine eight times before he took off the axles and made it into a cart."*

So fascinated, but I was still looking for a way out. He kept sharing and I kept getting lost in his tale. Ten minutes or so passed.

"... no I grew up in Zimbabwe. It was called Rhodesia then, but now I live in Houston."

"Oh, I've spent some time around Houston." I said. *"I was impressed with the forests in that area."* I responded, still aware of the nagging noise within my head keeping time.

"… no, New Zealand's climate is like that of a Pacific Isle, Australia is more hot and dry … "

I noticed my body still holding on to the ghost of an intention to be doing something. I breathed into the last of it and let it go. He had taken me to the edge of new lands and was offering his hand to walk me through them.

"Screw it!" I affirmed and, closing my computer, I got up and moved over to the open chair at his table. *"Do you mind if I sit?"*

"Not at all." He smiled.

I could see the Southern Cross in the sky.

Self-Love is giving yourself permission to be where your heart is leading you. It's not about figuring out what's good and loving for you, it's jumping right into the moment that wonder shows up in. You can't schedule loving yourself. You have to set aside your appointment book and follow where your attraction takes you.

I love my body
and appreciate
all that it has
endured for me. I
am now willing
and able to care
for it, tend to
its suffering,
and serve as the
channel for setting
it free.

WHAT I DID FOR LOVE

"If you want to see the love of your life, look in the mirror."
... *Byron Katie*

Cleansing is a natural part of healing. Whatever we're holding onto needs to be released and in its passing it is common to feel uncomfortably, unfamiliar with the process.

As we become more aware of the magnificence we are, we rediscover how deeply we love ourselves and when ready, we're guided to act on it.

Questioning toxic beliefs and the indigestible thinking that supports them, opens us to the possibility of change. We actualize this new release through simple, supportive actions: noticing the simple needs we've previously ignored or resisted, venturing out from our protective shells to explore empowering attractions, and nourishing our bodies with healthy foods, treatments and exercise.

The mental, emotional and physical limitations we cling to are all interrelated; letting go of one triggers the release of others. In our willingness to love ourselves our body shows us plainly the havoc these toxic beliefs have wrought within us along with what we're holding onto that suspends their liberation.

The initial pain, fear and discomfort we face in caring for ourselves is legitimate suffering. It's our opportunity for liberation; the body's reprieve from the trauma and distress we've suffered while preparing for regeneration.

I unconditionally accept myself as I am. I have no business letting your opinion get in the way of how Spirit leads me. In fact, my judgment of me carries just as little weight.

NONSTICK ESTEEM

"There are two things for which animals can be envied: they know nothing of the future; or of what people say about them."

… Voltaire

Terry Cole-Whitaker's book, *"What You Think of Me Is None of My Business"* says it all in the title.

Peace of mind is knowing we're whole and esteemed just as we are, no matter what we do or how we're perceived. It's a simple truth that everyone shares, but few seem to accept and enjoy the freedom of it.

As Spiritual Beings, nothing real or substantial can ever be added to or taken from us. So no matter what happens to us, nothing really happens to us.

What we experience as loss, fear and pain is due to our sense of attachment to the stories we believe about our relationships and roles. We share this human experience as a collective drama, awakening us to who we are and the wisdom of embracing it.

Our Being empowers us to accept that the only relationship leading to peace and understanding is the one that eventually dissolves between who we think we're becoming and who we really are.

When objectifying myself as someone in transition, I include my self with everyone else who could have opinions about me. Gratefully I know that what we think about me is none of my business.

*I am whole
and complete
eternally, while
my perception of
this is constantly
changing. The
former is my
reality. The latter
is my art.*

Portrait Of The Artist

"Trying to define yourself is like trying to bite your own teeth."

... Alan Watts

It's no wonder that trying to be a better person can seem a daunting task. The problem lies not in the methods but the intention itself. Look at a newborn baby. Is it possible that anything so beautiful could be improved upon?

We have to work every moment to ignore our perfection just to maintain the belief that we're flawed or missing something that we need to make us better. It is as if, through our minds, in painting a portrait of our life, we project ourselves into the painting. Thus having lost touch with ourselves, our power and our creativity through this act, we then frustratingly seek our recovery within the canvas itself. All the while forgetting to look back and see who is painting the picture.

When our world seems out of order, askew in its priorities, a difficult and painful place to live in, we ask ourselves, *"What's the solution? Do I need to heal my past, raise my self-esteem, work harder to change the future? Perhaps a stroke here, a little color there or a whole new canvas altogether?"*

The painting is fine the way it is, just climb out of it. We are not whom we think or feel or paint ourselves as. We're the ones holding the brush.

*I am grateful
for the lifelong
opportunity to love
and care for one
preciously innocent
soul. I give my
hand, my heart,
my attention to
me.*

COURAGE TO BE

"Every blade of grass has its Angel that bends over it and whispers, 'Grow, grow.'"

... *The Talmud*

Open your eyes and see. Are you missing the most precious, wondrous miracle of all? Dare to take a glimpse and feel your breath shudder deeply; leaping forth from great heart. Allow tears to stain your cheeks and give compassion free reign through your throat?

Look who's before you right now. The one who has postponed their own dreams in the face of others needs, who gave companionship to another's loneliness, who gave money, time and attention to raise hope, who, when hearing, *"judge and condemn"*, responded with forgiveness and understanding instead.

One who struggled with doubt and confusion but never gave in to despair, who believed in themselves in the midst of chaos and confusion and who glimpsed a shade of innocence within everything. One who in faith, tried their best, failed and then had the courage to try again.

One who has greeted the sun, played in the grass, swirled toes in the water, savored a first kiss, lingered over a sweet scent and known other delights.

Don't miss the most precious treasure of all. Turn to the mirror, slowly and still; gaze tenderly into the awe and mystery of you. You're the reason angels sing.

*I like me. I love
me. I believe in
me. I trust in my
nature, my choices,
and my actions.
I need no one's
approval to believe
in me or to believe
in you.*

WHO KNEW?

"You cannot be lonely if you like the person you are alone with."

... *Dr. Wayne Dyer*

During my wilderness experience in Alaska, I hated myself. I could hardly stay in my skin, while grievously facing the collapse of my attachments to others for self-worth and acceptance.

In the midst of losing my marriage, sense of place and outer security, I fought desperately and futilely; fabricating reasons to keep my head above the psychic waters. And when I lost contact with the "I" I had always believed myself to be, I spun out of control into an ever-descending pit of darkness and depression.

Then one morning after eighteen months of disjointed, unsubstantiated dread and hopelessness, I awoke to a ray of joy. Suddenly I knew and felt that I was OK being by myself, that I never am alone and that I enjoy my own company.

Since then many revelations have come, including the awareness of this love affair I'm having with myself. I realize now I couldn't love me because I was too weary from the busyness of protecting the me I pretended to be.

Now I listen, and question my desires and aversions, because I've got a lot to catch up on. How could I ever have failed to notice how compellingly extraordinary I am?

Transformation

I love greatly,
because I can.
Everyone and
everything lies
within the sphere
of my compassion.

BIG LOVE

"He drew a circle that shut me out-
Heretic, rebel a thing to flout.
But love and I had wit to win:
We drew a circle that took him in!"

... Edwin Markham

No one can ever limit our experience, nor shut us out of their world. We may believe the contrary when someone turns against us, betrays a trust, isolates or excludes us, but who has really been left out?

In truth they've done nothing to us, but to themselves. Our terrain is as large as it's ever been. It's their world that has diminished.

Real separation is not possible. To do so by closing off our hearts and shutting down awareness, is pure fantasy. And we pay a high premium for it, in depleted life force and increased suffering.

If it's insane for our brother or sister to suppress their joy forming pain over petty and ignorantly interpreted circumstance, then how wise is it for us to rise to the bait of their foolishness?

This is especially strange when we realize that we have the gift all along to help raise their true intention to feel safe. Someone can attempt to shut us out by wrapping themselves up in denial and ignorance, but we can still encircle and embrace them in love. Love is our natural affinity for each other and no one can ever take that away from us. We can only fail to see it.

*I believe in me
and in you. I trust
in Divine Love to
show us what is
kind, freeing and
true. I applaud
the perfect way our
lives play out.*

CENTER STAGE

"Make no more stories. Make no more drama. Make no more pain."
                                                            ... Dale Blackford

"Why can't he be _____? Why can't she see _____?" Fill in the blanks. It's the age-old story of human relations, the same drama that plays out today like an original performance.

The drama keeps repeating itself not for any wanting of heart in the players. The glitch is in the script. By accepting the belief *that we're caught in the need to change inferior circumstance* rather than following where it leads, we repeat the familiar, tiring roles of victim to champion over the same belief *that we're caught in the need to change inferior circumstance.* It's a long running engagement with no end in sight, just as the playwright (ego) intended.

We don't have to accept this gig, nor listen to any advice that tells us what needs to happen to make us a Star.

Fire your outside booking agent. Trust your heartfelt leading to support you in finding opportunities that are a natural fit. In being true to yourself you are free to appreciate your castmate(s), their talents and the drama itself without getting tangled in the script.

Your light will spontaneously uplift the dialogue and redirect the action. And you'll never once regret the spotlights that you've shared.

I know what I
want when it
shows up before
me. The Universe
ever surprises
me with more
preposterous joy
than I could ever
justify or imagine.

COULD BE TRUE

"Be patient towards all that is unsolved in your heart. And try to love the questions themselves. Do not seek the answers that cannot be given you because you would not be able to live them.
And the point is to live everything.
So live the questions now, perhaps you will gradually, without noticing it, live along some distant day, into the answers."
... Rainer Maria Rilke

When we were little we wanted what we wanted when we wanted it. And if we didn't get it right away we became angry, sad or afraid.

This belief hasn't changed much for most of us since then, although as adults we've developed more efficient ways than nagging our parents for what we want: marketing, politicizing and manipulating situations, resources and people, to name a few.

Could it be true that what we need might not be what we think we want when we want it?

Could our thinking about the wanting and the getting be the very obstacle that's frustrating the life out of our dreams? Are we putting off grander possibilities with the belief that we're limited only to what we think we can successfully badger the universe for?

Could this same thinking be what keeps us from enjoying the wonder of what is right under our noses—intimacy with our partners, children and friends, the phenomenal beauty of the natural world, the symphony of human interaction and all that we can possibly imagine?

How could this be true? Question false beliefs, entertain what you have been missing, and see how shackles release while new possibilities take form.

I am not afraid
of what might
come out of me. I
would be terrified
if I could forever
keep it inside. It's
a blessing that I
leak.

FEARLESS IMMORTAL INVENTORY

"There's one way to find out if a man is honest - ask him. If he says, 'Yes,' you know he is a crook."

... *Groucho Marx*

I've learned that there are truths that don't often see the light of day. They are hidden away by a collective understanding that once they are let out, we won't be able to hide them anymore.

There are truths of our human experience that we fear to show others, though we all recognize them when we are alone.
They are:

- the doubts and fears I think and act upon contrary to my conscience.
- the shame of turning from faith in my possibilities to the predictability of what I've always known.
- how I choose to react compulsively from my prejudices, ignorance and self-interest.
- the arrogance with which I judge others by the norms I won't hold for myself.
- the self-righteousness with which I justify the indefensible.
- the convenient unconsciousness I accept when I am unwilling to face the hard truths that can free me.

This list is far from complete, however it's more than a good start. For by owning these truths I'm unburdened by the weight of their concealment, and inspired by new wisdom.

I'm released from whatever I no longer carry inside me. Everything in my human journey reflects the Love that Creation has invested in me.

*I am not who I
was. I am who
I now will be.
I am willing,
confident and
excited to know
the me who has
now shown up.*

I Gotta Be Me

"It takes courage to grow up and become who you really are."

... *e. e. cummings*

Much of our conversation isn't true. It's crafted around the intention to keep others distracted from seeing what we're hiding inside us.

We have past memories as innocent children, sharing openly what was in us, only to have parents, other children and adults use our offerings to punish, humiliate or confuse us.

As we grow older we notice that others practice this as well; spouting the safe and trite with occasional leakage of their true thoughts and feelings.

In business, politics, etc. this guardedness has developed into a legitimized language of deceit, that we call politically correct. Don't say what you mean, say what others won't challenge.

This martial practice has formed such an attitude of separateness that even the simplest to most intimate relationship often feels more like risk than opportunity.

Closing ourselves off can't erase the past or even filter out our experience of it, however, it does cut us off from knowing ourselves and our unexplored strengths and potential that vulnerability to life brings out in us.

When being true to ourselves as children, the consequences we faced appeared large. By revisiting them now as adults, like the house we grew up in, they might be a lot smaller than we remember.

Trust

TRUST

"She's pissing me off!" I ruminated.

"I hate it when she shuts down and closes me off without a word as to what she's feeling or thinking."

I had, once again, stumbled upon her upset. It began with me asking those questions about miscommunications, methodologies and general expectations. With each further step into my exploration of *"what's going on"* to *"what's expected"* to *"what's needed"*, her tone became harsher, her response more clipped.

Unaware of what I was feeling, but still irritated by it, I reacted, snapping back at her, *"What's going on with you? You're barking at me. At everything I say. I'm just trying to find out what you need from me, that's all. Please don't snap at me."*

"I'm sorry." She said. *"I didn't mean to do that."*

I went back to my room to finish what I had left undone, but all I could think of was how she might be feeling and the look on her face that warned, *"Don't ask."*

"I hate this." I kept thinking. *"I hate it when she gets upset and shuts me out. I don't do that to her ... I don't think? And even if I did, I would at least give her a clue about what's bothering me. Why does she have to shut me out anyways?"*

I recognized the conversation with myself. It's one I've replayed over and over again, and it never leaves me satisfied. Worse, it never gives me an answer that puts my mind and heart at peace.

However, it has shown me the way to the peace that I have been seeking. The utter futility of trying to change another person or situation, and my ridiculously flawed reasoning for attempting to, has forced me to see and accept the only obvious alternative—trust.

I really can't be certain of what is going on with me or anyone else, in any given situation, other than the most important understanding; that we are all created by, immersed within and dependent on the leading of a Mysterious Benevolence that transcends our understanding and perfectly orchestrates everything.

I can't fully trust my judgment of anything, but I can trust the Universal Stage upon which life plays. Because whether I like it or not, what needs to come out will be called into the light and what needs to remain hidden will stay unseen.

She left without saying *"goodnight"*. That hurts and confuses me. I don't know what is happening, but I can accept that it is happening—because it is.

Trust is not something that you give to anyone or anything. It's what you can rely on in everyone and everything. To not trust is to arrogantly assume that your perception cultivates reality, instead of the other way around. You cannot trust in your ability to make sense out of what you can so limitedly see, but you can trust in your rightful place (your Being) in the Limitlessness that runs it all so Perfectly.

I trust in the
Source of my
creation. When
lost I turn within
to the Wisdom
that urges
patience, until
more is revealed.

More Is Being Revealed

"I'm a skeptic, but highly open to persuasion."

... *Dale Blackford*

Along our unfolding spiritual journey we encounter many truths. The mystical ones of who we are, the nature of our universe, our purpose for being and so forth. Then there are the relative truths: how we attach to our thinking, the beliefs we form that limit us, how we project our frustration onto others and many more.

But in our awakening to the abundance of truths before us one stands out as most consistently empowering. It is that everything has purpose, meaning and its place within the unfolding Order of our Perfected Universe—no matter how it appears.

The foundation of faith is knowing that in the midst of what seems most convoluted, confusing, or desperate, we need only release our certainty about what we're seeing in order to view it from a wider, more friendly perspective.

We don't need to change the course of our lives, or even the habit of continuing to try. Spirit brings to us the truth of every lie standing between our beliefs and our freedom.

Ignorance and suffering cannot endure. Our Spirit is incorruptible, and we are part of an Order that mandates our joyous awakening within it. Enough said.

*I trust the world to
form itself around
my heart's desire
and my joyous
intention. I release
myself from trying
so hard to play the
game backwards.*

FREE AGENCY

"Don't get caught in the machine of the world—it is too exacting. By the time you get what you are seeking your nerves are gone, the heart is damaged, and the bones are aching. ... If you have joy you have everything so learn to be glad and contented ... Have happiness now."

... Paramahansa Yogananda

It's difficult having to mold ourselves around circumstance in order to fit in with the world.

Society rarely accepts us as we are, but measures us by what we've done. The more we buy into this standard the greater are its demands.

Peer pressure to develop an acceptable image begins early with cliques, fashion, body shaping, language, opinions and other rituals.

It continues on into adulthood with posturing through parenting and careers, cultivating contacts and relationships, accumulating money, things and managing their excess, courting recognition, power and status.

At some point though, the game either ends or slows to completion. In the realization of its withdrawal, we are confronted with the heavy toll it has taken on us; having had to manipulate our innocence into the cunningness of a player.

Losing our place in the game can bring up anger, denial and grief. However, as it recedes it is replaced by the deepening joy and freedom of never having to strive again to make ourselves into something other than we are.

The question now is, *"Could it be that playing the game is how I avoid freedom, and that how I work to make my life better is the very cause of my unease?"*

*I step out from
the security of past
circumstances into
the space of what
has yet to be. The
ground is firm
below me, but my
face is raised to the
sky.*

HIGH WIRED

"Life is being on the wire, everything else is just waiting."

… Karl Wallenda

Every moment we have the opportunity to step into life and face the wonder and mystery of where it leads. Like a violinist anticipating the conductor's cue, we await, prepared in this moment, so that when the baton beckons, we're ready to perform.

The basic skills we need for meeting this moment are simple: faith, willingness, attentiveness and curiosity.

Faith provides the backdrop; a safety net and personal assurance that no matter what shows up, we're able to meet it and be richer for the experience.

Willingness guides our mind and heart in following through on our faith. Familiarity with what we encounter won't cut it. We need to be willing to be intimate with it—to step into the living waters that flow around us.

Attentiveness is the quality that allows us to see expanded possibilities through the focus of our presence. This deepens our awareness of Universal Synchronicity, heightening our appreciation for living more fully.

And curiosity draws us into the full wonder and acceptance of our nature, to live each moment's offering in spontaneity, joy and peace.

Life effuses warm, full invitation. Go ahead and walk through the door. The party is waiting on your arrival.

I jump into life
with both feet,
fearless of where
I land, faithful
to my stance;
firm and true.
A foundation
of substantial
wonders supports
all of my shaky
expectations.

POSITIVELY FED UP

"You can't always get what you want. But if you try sometime, you just might find, you get what you need."

... *Mick Jagger & Keith Richards, The Rolling Stones*

Life can appear as the old bait and switch. We crave the latest toy, only to quickly tire of it, find the right job, only to look for another. Our soulmate shows up, only to discover they're soon looking like our ex.

Changing toys, jobs, partners or whatever we're dissatisfied with rarely changes anything. At best it gives us a break between fulfilling our next expectations, where we can go through the same elation to deflation process once again.

At some point it begins to dawn on us that the problem might not be out there, but within us. Then, what to do?

Actually, when we begin to see this frustrating reality we are already allowing outcomes to expand. Satisfaction with life is always a present possibility. Even the pattern of striving for what we think we want, that continually never fulfills us, helps us see and separate the compulsion of our doing, from the heart of our intention.

It awakens us, because just in recognizing the futility of chasing empty expectations, we are then freed to turn our attention to what we truly desire and need. And like a grand, gracious Host, Life serves up more than we would ever possibly imagine.

"Oh do try this. You will love it."

I trust implicitly
in the Order of
Spirit and my
place within It. I
accept the people
and circumstances
in my life just as
they are, just as
I am moved to
relate with them.

In You I Trust

"When I walk on the beach to watch the sunset I do not call out, 'A little more orange over to the right, please,' or 'Would you mind giving us less purple in the back?' No, I enjoy the always-different sunsets as they are. We do well to do the same with people we love."

... *Carl Rogers*

If we saw others more like sunsets—cosmic happenings outside our sphere of influence—we might be more accepting of each other. However, within the understanding that we can use persuasion and manipulation to change circumstances, we believe we can and ought to employ these tactics.

This perspective could only be true if we were actually able to perceive the whole of anything. The truth is that we see little but the surface of what is before us, including our effect upon it.

A new butterfly labors to free itself from the cocoon. We could be moved to ease its Herculean task by pulling apart the prison and releasing it from its struggle. But by so doing we corrupt the butterfly's transition—it's wings and new body left weakened from the aborted effort that would have strengthened them. Our intention, though seemingly noble, lacks awareness.

Each of us is like that butterfly and sunset—beautiful, capable and on course, even when the situation, choice or behavior doesn't make sense?

We need only love and accept all that we don't understand, in faith that our Spirit can and will make our participation in change clearly apparent if and when its needed.

AFTERWORD

The life of splendor that you have only glimpsed in your dreams is lying right before you now, in full expression. It is with sweet hope and in blissful gratitude that I offer this book to guide you along your way. Enjoy the ride my friend. Every part of this journey will take you directly to the brilliance that is you.

Dale

ABOUT THE AUTHOR

Dale Blackford is an Awakened Soul and Master Teacher who facilitates the shift from the pain and frustration of trying to become better, to realizing the immediate joy and freedom of knowing your perfection, exactly as you are. He helps others connect with their brilliance and immediate potential. A no-nonsense visionary, Dale believes in the urgency of experiencing present moment bliss. His teaching, coaching and workshops are simply and extraordinarily empowering.

The end of suffering is at the foundation of Dale's teachings. He is intimately familiar with the intensity of this struggle and how it leads directly to peace. Release from compulsive thinking about the past, the future and problem solving, opens into immediate access to present moment fulfillment, where you are not only shown the way, but escorted by spirit into the full experience of living it.

Dale is a speaker, writer, radio broadcaster, teacher and open channel who allows Spirit free access through him. He is the father of two beautiful daughters and grandfather of a magnificent grandson. An American citizen, Dale presently lives in the Greater Toronto Area where he has been exploring his innate Canadian-ness.

The producer of several publications and CD's, Dale also hosts a weekly radio show, *"The Heart of Being"*, on Unity FM Radio (www. unity.fm). He can be seen on youtube.com by clicking on http://www. youtube.com/watch?v=jrYtDNjVnfY

You can contact Dale at www.daleblackford.com, dale@ daleblackford.com or 716.425.8979.